U N L I K E L Y   S P I R I T U A L   H E R O E S

UNLIKELY
spiritual
heroes

BRENNAN R. HILL

ST. ANTHONY MESSENGER PRESS
Cincinnati, Ohio

Scripture passages have been taken from *New Revised Standard Version Bible*, copyright
©1989 by the Division of Christian Education of the National Council of the Churches of
Christ in the U.S.A., and used by permission. All rights reserved.

Cover and book design by Mark Sullivan

LIBRARY OF CONGRESS CATALOGING-IN-PUBLICATION DATA
Hill, Brennan.
Unlikely spiritual heroes / Brennan R. Hill.
p. cm.
Includes bibliographical references (p.   ) and index.
ISBN 978-0-86716-924-9 (pbk. : alk. paper) 1. Catholics—Biography. 2. Catholic
Church—History. I. Title.

BX4651.3.H55 2010
282.092'2—dc22
[B]
2010000851

ISBN 978-0-86716-924-9

Published by St. Anthony Messenger Press
28 W. Liberty St.
Cincinnati, OH 45202
www.SAMPBooks.org

Printed in the United States of America.

Printed on acid-free paper.

10 11 12 13 14   5 4 3 2 1

To my wife and hero, Marie, who, as a mediator,
has been so dedicated to peaceful conflict resolution
and to seeking justice for the children of divorce.

contents

Much gratitude to the librarians at Xavier University, Ohio Link, and the Athenaeum of Ohio for so graciously helping me find resources. Many thanks to my wife, Marie, for her valuable critiques and proofreading, and to Mary Curran-Hackett for her splendid editing.

Unlikely Heroes

No one is born a hero. Heroism seems to be a coming together of background, gifts, a mysterious and providential calling to meet a challenge, and a courageous and tenacious response.

Most heroes start off like the rest of us: as ordinary and flawed individuals, searching for their true selves and for what they should do with their lives. Then suddenly they are asked to step up and do great things for others. In the case of a true hero, the response is selfless, inspiring, even breathtaking.

The eight figures here are indeed unlikely heroes, in that anyone who knew them early on would not have guessed the heights to which they would climb, the amazing efforts they would make to bring peace and justice to their world.

Jean Donovan was a flamboyant businesswoman who rode a Harley to work; both Helen Prejean and Dorothy Stang were traditional nun-schoolteachers; Pedro Arrupe dropped out of medical school to become a Jesuit and was sent to Japan to guide novices; Thomas Merton wandered Europe as a motherless child and dropped out of college after fathering a child; Maximilian Kolbe was a sickly and overly pious Franciscan, thought to be eccentric by many of his confreres; and Joseph Bernardin was the bookish son of Italian immigrants, who entered the clerical world when the Irish dominated the hierarchy. John Paul II was a young actor with his sights set on a life on the stage—he had no idea it would be the world's stage where he would shine the brightest. But all of them became heroes—unlikely—but heroes just the same. If they could do it, there is indeed hope for all of us.

A Trilogy on Heroes

Well, now I have written a whole trilogy about twenty-four of my heroes. What started with a suggestion from my wife, Marie, to incorporate heroes into my theology classes at Xavier University, grew into entire courses on heroes and exciting presentations in parishes. And now I have completed three volumes, featuring twenty-four outstanding people.

The first volume, 8 *Spiritual Heroes: Their Search for God,* explored the lives of individuals who pursued God in unique and inspiring ways (people as diverse as Mohandas Gandhi and Edith Stein). The second, 8 *Freedom Heroes: Changing the World With Faith,* dealt with people who made heroic efforts to free themselves and to free others (ranging from Nelson Mandela to Corrie ten Boom). And now, this final volume looks at eight Catholics, who were dedicated to following their church's rich social teachings on peace and justice.

Meet the Heroes

The order in which the heroes are treated reflects an inverse hierarchy, according to her or his title in the church. They are all "people of God," and dedicated to the teachings and example of Jesus Christ. First there is a laywoman, who left a lucrative profession in Cleveland to walk with and advocate for the poor and oppressed in El Salvador. Jean Donovan, along with three religious sisters, was perceived to be "dangerous," just as Jesus had been in his time. The four women were sexually assaulted, murdered, and buried in a shallow grave by government troops.

Then there are two religious sisters. One, Helen Prejean, has been a formidable opponent of the death penalty and has accompanied some men on the lonely and frightening path to execution. The other sister is Dorothy Stang, who gave thirty years of her life to the service of the indigenous poor in the Brazilian rain forests, defending their rights to the land, and protecting their environment from greedy and violent ranchers and loggers. Dorothy was murdered in 2004, with her Gospels in hand and love in her heart.

There are three male religious. First, there is Jesuit Pedro Arrupe, who led his Society of Jesus into the era of Vatican II reform and taught them to serve poor students and be strong advocates for peace and justice. A number of Jesuits were willing to sacrifice their lives following his leadership. The next is Thomas Merton, a Trappist monk and well-known spiritual writer, who later in life turned his pen to passionately oppose war and be a strong advocate for justice. And finally, there is Franciscan Maximilian Kolbe, a powerful leader in his community and a tireless publisher who came to face a brutal Nazi regime in his homeland, Poland. He, too, was labeled "dangerous" for his stress on love over hate, and for his harboring of refugees, including thousands of Jews, in his monastery. Kolbe was ultimately sent to Auschwitz. He courageously stepped forward to take the place of a condemned man, and was thus placed in solitary confinement without food or water until his agonizing death.

There is a cardinal among our heroes, Joseph Bernardin. He helped shape the United States bishops' conference into a collegial body that was a force in this country on such issues as economic justice and nuclear disarmament. He also taught us that ethical issues were varied but as connected as a seamless garment.

And finally, we turn to a pope, John Paul II, one of the most influential religious leaders in our time. During his long papacy, the Holy Father was a strong and intrepid defender of human dignity and nonviolence in his native Poland and throughout the world.

In these three volumes I have tried to develop what I call a "biographical theology." This is a theology which arises out of human experience, a "theology from below." It is a theology that is not only of the mind, but of the heart and it moves individuals to action.

Spiritual Heroes for Peace and Justice

In my first volume, I demonstrated the wide range of images and experiences of God that arose out of the lives of people from different religions and areas. In the second volume, I explored the many facets of personal and social freedom, whether it be the freedom from slavery, hatred, unjust work laws, the oppression of women or of the disabled, racial prejudice, or even oppression within the church itself.

In this volume we discover that injustice and violence come in many different forms: poverty, endangering the environment, torture, execution, the nuclear arms race, poor health care, and political oppression. All of these ethical issues are interrelated and our heroes here demonstrate how Jesus, his gospel, and the Catholic church's social teachings call us to a mission of peace and justice.

chapter one

Jean Donovan

Her body was pulled out of a shallow grave in a remote rural area of El Salvador, along with the bodies of three missionary nuns. The four women had been stripped, sexually assaulted, mutilated, and shot. Jean was the layperson among the missionaries, and she had just returned to this war-torn country from a visit home, fully aware that she was putting her life on the line in order to accompany the poor in their horrific suffering. Jean Donovan, a sparkling young woman from Cleveland, would now be added to the list of the martyrs of El Salvador.

Early Years

Jean was born in 1953 just as the Korean War was winding down, during the stable Eisenhower years. Her mother, Patricia, was the daughter of a business tycoon, Jay Murphy; her father was a successful engineer. Jean grew up with her older brother in the quiet Cleveland suburbs. At five Jean was given a palomino and over the next ten years became an accomplished horsewoman, winning numerous trophies.

Jean's teen years coincided with the tumultuous sixties: civil rights demonstrations, riots, assassinations, and the struggles over Vietnam. Her life in the public schools and a traditional Catholic parish insulated her from much of the controversy. At the same time, Jean was the maverick in the family. She was a tomboy with rough edges, and she had a determined, independent streak. She was a strong young woman whose vulnerabilities were mostly kept hidden.

Jean shared her family's conservative Republican values, their support for Richard Nixon, and their contempt for protesters. At college, Jean continued riding and eventually settled on an economics major and a goal of developing a successful career in finance. Jean earned her master's in economics from Case Western and was hired by Arthur Andersen, the largest accounting firm in the nation, as a management consultant. Jean was at the top of her game: She had a fine salary, her own apartment overlooking Lake Michigan, a new car, and her own Harley to ride around town.

Ireland

At a Christmas office party, Jean suddenly got the feeling that something was wrong, that she wasn't where she should be. She took a vacation and booked a trip to Ireland where, during her college foreign exchange year she had been first jarred to look at herself and her goals. The city of Cork, with its tiny houses, simple food, and bleak landscape, had been a culture shock for Jean. For the first time she met people who valued personal relationships more than material things. It was there that she met an Irish priest, Michael Crowley, who would become her lifelong confidant and mentor.

Crowley had spent ten years as a missionary in the slums of Trujillo, Peru, and had a strong sense of solidarity with the poor as well as radical ideas about the redistribution of wealth. He was a man of wit and wisdom, who awakened Jean to the plight of the oppressed poor in Latin America. He seems to have legitimized Jean's calling to do missionary work, one that she had harbored secretly in her heart. Crowley invited Jean and other young people to visit the elderly, the sick, and mental patients. She began to empathize with them and see the world and herself in a new way. Jean discovered suffering and learned that she could reach out with compassion and bring joy into the lives of others. Crowley would tell Jean and the others: "It's better to do something than to give up something."[1]

Now Jean was back at Crowley's door as a successful businesswoman, and yet as an individual longing to transform her life. They spent long evenings by a turf fire, drinking Irish whiskey and discussing life and Jean's search for meaning.

Return to America

On her return to Cleveland, Jean began to work as a volunteer with inner-city kids and continued to have discussions, now with the local parish priest. At one of their meetings he gave her a brochure about a mission in El Salvador. A light went on: That is what Jean wanted to do! She told her parents she was going to quit her job and work as a missionary. She applied for training with the Maryknoll Order, telling them: "I have a gut feeling that my main motivation to be a missionary is a true calling from God."[2]

Jean trained for four months with the Maryknolls, where she seemed to some loud, headstrong, and unorthodox, to the extent that some in charge had reservations about approving her. She finally passed muster, however, and became part of the Maryknoll family.

On to Central America

After Maryknoll, Jean traveled to Guatemala for language training and then on to El Salvador in the spring of 1979. She would be separated from family, friends, and her boyfriend, Doug Cable, for several years. She would enter a country plagued by unemployment, undernourishment, and poor housing. A dozen or so rich families controlled the land, the military, and the government. Those in opposition, whether extreme leftist terrorists, urban guerrillas, or members of peaceful grassroots organizations were all branded subversives and communists and oppressed by the military. The church, which had long been on the side of the rich and powerful, was now shifting allegiance to the poor. Priests were organizing small faith communities and promoting liberation theology in order to empower the people. As a result, many priests were targeted as subversives. One of the first to be assassinated was the Jesuit and beloved friend of Oscar Romero, Rutilio Grande. After that, death squads were formed from the security forces and flyers went out saying, "Be a patriot—kill a priest." The United States sent the Salvadoran government huge sums of money to combat terrorists. Instead the funds were used to suppress any resistance to the brutal oppression. Jean was thrown into this boiling cauldron of violence and suffering.

Arrival in Central America

The month Jean arrived in Central America had been filled with violence. The army had opened fire on young people at a demonstration, killing twenty-three and wounding dozens of others; fourteen teens had been killed on another march. Jean went to El Salvador where she attended the funeral of a priest who had been shot while at the altar.[3] Jean was frightened, disoriented, and wondering if she had made a mistake. She wrote: "I keep getting frustrated and wonder what I am doing here as opposed to being married and living at lollipop acres...."[4]

La Libertad

Jean's mission was in La Libertad, a town on the Pacific Ocean, where she joined two priests and two nuns. Her mentor and eventually close friend was Ursuline sister Dorothy Kazel. Dorothy was athletic and vivacious. She came to El Salvador in 1974. Previously she taught children and worked with inner-city kids with emotional and drug problems.[5]

Jean's main jobs were to distribute food to a larger community of harvesters and to keep the books for the mission. She was quite a sight, riding around on her Honda motorcycle, with a guitar strapped to her back, and enthusiastically prepared to offer people any services needed. Still she was filled with doubts, lacked self-confidence, and felt that the people she served had much to teach her about courage, dignity, and generosity. She wrote to a friend, "It seems that you're here to be ministered to a lot more than to minister."[6]

In the course of her work, Jean had the opportunity to be associated with Archbishop Romero, and was deeply impressed with his humble leadership and dedication to the cause of the poor. Romero had been a pious, conservative bishop, who stayed out of politics until his close friend Rutilio Grande was gunned down. Realizing his own government was behind the repression of his people, he decided to stand up for the oppressed. He traveled the country compassionately listening to the cries of his people. Romero put his life on the line, regularly denouncing the repression. He was convinced that "the world which the church ought to serve is for us the world of the poor."[7] At the same time, he renounced the violence on both sides. He became an important hero of Jean's. When he came to the parish, she would bake his favorite chocolate chip cookies and keep him supplied with them at his residence.

On breaks Jean enjoyed visits from her family or her boyfriend, Doug. Though the visitors did not see much violence on their "protected tours," the situation was badly deteriorating. Romero exposed the armed forces as the center of the repression and in 1980 he appealed to President Carter to stop military aid. He knew well by this time that he was on the list of those to be eliminated.

Death of the Archbishop
Romero continued to document the hundreds of murder victims and denounced the killers from the pulpit in his national broadcast weekly. In his March 23 sermon, he cried out to the security forces to stop the repression. That was it for the military—Romero was giving orders to the troops. An assassination plan was put in place and the very next day Romero was fatally shot through the heart while saying Mass.

The outcry was enormous and there was a great outpouring of grief and sorrow from the many *campesinos*. Jean was deeply saddened and wrote, "He was fearlessly honest. He lived a simple life of continual forgiveness and love, he was the friend of the weak and the poor...."[8] Jean accompanied Romero's body to the cathedral, guarded the open casket in the cathedral and stood by the body during the bombing and shooting outside. Afraid for her own life, she remained calm. Romero was her hero and she wanted to be by him. Now Jean was convinced that God had sent her to this place and wanted her to stay there no matter what.[9]

After Romero's death, two Maryknoll sisters, Ita Ford and Carla Piette, came to El Salvador from Chile, where they had struggled against the repression of the infamous General Pinochet. Ita was infuriated by the cruelty she witnessed in Chile, and her experience there prepared her to deal with the horrors of El Salvador. The missions were in her blood. Her uncle was a bishop who died in a communist prison in China. She was a well educated, accomplished writer and a down-to-earth woman who could enjoy a cigarette and a drink. Carla was a tall, striking woman, with an attractive personality and unlimited energy. In Chile she had shown remarkable endurance and courage in defense of the poor.[10]

Both Ita and Carla were wise veterans and became role models for Jean. Initially they were sent to Chalatenango in the northeast to work with the many refugees fleeing from the terror and violence. Meanwhile, Jean kept careful note of the persecutions of the people in her journal and sent tapes to Father Crowley about the many atrocities. She helped with the horrific task of assembling body parts and corpses to be decently buried, even though this was against the law. Of course, the death squads watched and took note of this disobedience. One death moved her deeply, that of young Armando Avalae, the church sacristan with whom she had become very close. Jean was distraught at the many friends and parishioners killed. She wrote to Crowley that she felt like a coward because she did not want to die. At the same time, she steadfastly held to her principles of nonviolence.[11]

In August 1980 tragedy struck. Ita and Carla often transported refugees and priests through the hills to safety. One day they were transporting a young refugee across a river when a flash flood caught their Jeep. Carla drowned. Ita was saved only because Carla pushed her out of the vehicle. The accident left Ita both physically and emotionally exhausted.[12]

Jean ministered to the suffering Ita and offered to take Carla's place in Chalatenango. Carla's death convinced Jean that her place was with the poor of El Salvador. There would be no turning back. Maryknoll instead chose to replace Carla with a seasoned veteran from Nicaragua, Maura Clark. Maura was an Irish nun who grew up in New York City. She loved to dance the Irish jig. She was known for her generosity and often gave her money and personal possessions to the poor. She was known to have saved some people from torture and death during the brutal regime of Somoza in Nicaragua through courageously confronting the authorities.[13]

A Vacation

In September, Jean took a whirlwind vacation trip to see Doug and her family. Everyone noticed that she had changed, and from her stories it became evident that Jean was in serious danger. Doug and her family tried to persuade her not to go back, but to no avail. Even Father Crowley could not dissuade her, though he made it clear that she would be tortured and killed. She was now determined to face whatever came. Jean simply could not abandon the people who needed her. She wrote to a friend, "Several times I have decided to leave El Salvador. I almost could except for the children, the poor, bruised victims of this insanity. Who would care for them? Whose heart could be so staunch as to favor the reasonable thing in a sea of their tears and loneliness? Not mine, dear friend, not mine."[14] She had done much soul-searching at home, and praying and struggling at Maryknoll, but there was a resolute calmness as she boarded the plane to return to El Salvador. Her brother anguished: "She's not coming back."[15]

Return to the Mission

Jean got right into the action. The focus was rescuing refugees, especially in Chalatenango where Ita and Maura were stationed. Jean drove a van to transport many of them. She was more serene and self-confident now, apparently clearer on her mission in life. She was more able to overcome her fears through faith and trust in her God. She now was more in touch with her true self and that gave her a deep sense of peace. Jean had realized what it meant to die to self, to gain the spirituality of the poor, and to be "ministered to" by the oppressed.

By October the death squads were moving into Chalatenango to terrorize the people, killing and cutting up bodies with machetes. The oligarchy was determined to wipe out any farmers or workers who were organizing for change and branded them all communists. The attitude of the military was that guerrillas are fish that swim in peasant waters, so if you kill the peasants you get the guerrillas along the way.[16] The peasants were fleeing their homes and farms and thereby creating a food shortage. Ita, Maura, and Jean were now deeply involved in transporting food to the starving people.

On one occasion a distraught mother looking for her son (who had been taken by the police) came to Jean and Ita for help. They located a burial site. When it was opened, they saw the face of the boy. The mother was consoled that she found her son and knew he was now with God. Ita, however, looked at the face and was deeply unsettled, as though she was staring at her own death. In one month, she would be in a similar shallow grave.

Soon after this incident, a notice was posted on the door of the parish house in Chalatenango. It pictured a human head with a knife in it and read: "This is what will happen to anyone who comes to this house because the priests and nuns are communists."[17] The local authorities had decided that the missionaries were inciting the people to resist the government and were supporting guerrillas. The three women began to see that their solidarity with their people was bringing them into the circle of death in that area.

In November, Jean wrote Senator Edward Kennedy and told him American military aid was being used to torture and murder oppressed people. She informed him that the church was also being persecuted because it was the only voice against oppression. She decried the atrocities she witnessed and asked for his assistance.

Early in December Jean and some of the other missionaries were invited to have dinner at the house of American ambassador Robert White. White was charmed by Jean and had a long discussion with her about what was going on in the States as well as in El Salvador. He later wrote that Jean had apparently become radicalized by her experience with the poor, was feeling the injustice of it all, and was dedicated to bringing relief to the people. The guests stayed overnight because of the dangers on the dark roads, and the next morning went cheerfully to run some errands before going to the airport to pick up Ita and Maura, who had attended a Maryknoll conference in Nicaragua. At the closing liturgy, Ita read a passage from one of Romero's sermons:

> Christ invites us not to fear persecution, brothers and sisters,...because believe me, he who is committed to the poor must share the same fate as the poor; and in El Salvador we know what that fate signifies: it is to disappear, to be tortured, to be captive and to be found dead by the side of the road.[18]

The passage would indeed turn out to be prophetic.

Ita, Maura, and two other nuns set out to return to El Salvador, but could not get flights together so Ita and Maura stayed back for the next flight. Jean and Dorothy met the first two, took them to La Libertad, and then returned to the airport to pick up Ita and Maura. Members of the National Guard were waiting as well. The plane landed at 7:00 PM; at the same time in Chalatenango a man gave a piece of paper to one of the parish staff where Ita and Maura worked. The paper was a list of names, which included those two nuns and the man said: "Here is a list of people we are going to kill—and today, this very night, we will begin."[19] When the two nuns arrived they were picked up by Jean and Dorothy in the white van. The four drove off—it would be the last time they would all be seen alive. Their murders would cause a national and international explosion, one that moved many in El Salvador to think that liberation was perhaps on the way.[20]

The Death of Four Martyrs

A report from the trial of one of the guardsmen reported that several guardsmen were told to put on civilian clothes to prepare for an assignment. At the airport they received their orders. They got out of their Jeep near an airport tollbooth, stopped a white van with four women in it, got in, and drove off. At a deserted area, they were ordered to shoot the women, but first they abused the women sexually. This was done because the women were so-called subversives.[21]

Two mornings later, a farmer told his parish priest about a fresh grave containing the bodies of the four women. The priest contacted the archdiocese who called the American embassy. Word spread quickly to the parish house in La Libertad and to the Maryknoll headquarters in Washington, D.C. On the home front, Jean's family received word—first that she and three others were missing and later about the discovery of the four bodies. They were prepared for the worst. Senator Kennedy called and offered to help. Ambassador White received a call at the airport and immediately sought out the site.

At the grave, a *campesino* told White that two nights before he had heard shots and that a milkman had discovered the bodies next to the road in the morning. Soon after, the national guard arrived and ordered the locals to bury the women. White was sure that this must be the missionaries and wanted them dug up. The farmers were afraid to do this without permission of the local authority. Papers were signed and the grisly business of digging and removing the corpses began. Jean's body was dragged out first, naked, her face blown off by a bullet through the back of the head. Maura was next, then Dorothy, and finally Ita, her tiny body broken and smashed. The bodies were covered with branches and the group knelt in prayer.

White was furious and fumed at the local authorities for not reporting this incident. He simply answered that this was an everyday occurrence, no different from the hundreds of other deaths in the area. Later White was outraged that the national guard, who had presided over the burial, did not notify him or make any effort to find the burned-out white van, which one of the sisters easily discovered near the airport. White was insistent that American military and economic assistance be stopped until these matters and many others involving human rights were resolved. Washington sent a team of investigators, but they received little cooperation from the military, who believed that such actions were a necessary part of the "dirty war."[22] A cover-up was in the works.

Jean's and the others' families were notified when the women were identified. They were heartbroken at the news. Ita and Maura, in keeping with the Maryknoll custom, were buried among the people they served in Chalatenango. Their families, unbelieving, watched the whole event on television. After a moving ceremony in La Libertad, where the caskets of Jean and Dorothy were passed through the congregation amid loud applause, their bodies were flown back to the States for family funerals and burials.

One of Jean's friends captured her spirit by imagining the scene of the abduction:

> I can see Jean being pulled off the road by a bunch of army guys or whatever, and her saying, "How dare you? Do you know who I am?" I can see her facing a band of guys with machine guns and saying, "You don't know who the hell you're talking to. How dare you. I'm Jean Donovan. I'm working with the missionaries. Let that woman go!..." I can just see her trying to take control, trying to get a hold of the situation and boss people around—and getting her head blown off for her trouble.[23]

The Cover-up

It has been almost thirty years since Jean and her fellow missionaries were so brutally murdered, their bodies thrown by the wayside. Many questions still remain. How could the American government allow a military force, in part trained and armed by us, destroy the lives of these four saintly women and so many other innocent people? How could American officials participate in an elaborate cover-up, which hid evidence and threw suspicion on the victims themselves? How could a young woman and her three companions dedicated to peace and justice be dealt with so violently and unjustly?

The cover-up began during the first days following the deaths of the four women.[24] Although Archbishop Rivera Damas denounced the security forces for the crime, the government was adamant about its innocence.[25] Bill Ford, Ita's brother and an experienced lawyer, was intent on seeing that justice be done. He soon learned that neither government was interested in the case and that these deaths were merely an inconvenience to American policy. The American government, under both the Carter and Reagan administrations, had a fixed policy in El Salvador, and that policy was not released. Though military aid was suspended, it was resumed in a matter of days. When an official report was released it showed circumstantial evidence of complicity by the security forces. When members of the families went to the State Department in early December, they were told that no progress had been made in the investigation. They later found out that Ambassador White had been filing daily reports on a cover-up. Bill Ford reported that he received no information from the State Department and that his calls were not returned.

On December 28, an American reporter went to El Salvador to investigate the killings. He vanished; his skeleton turned up two years later.

When the Reagan administration took over, the oligarchy of El Salvador held champagne parties and the cover-ups intensified. Jeane Kirkpatrick, the U.S. ambassador to the United Nations, asserted that the government was unequivocally not responsible for the killings, and that the nuns were not just nuns, but political activists. She said they worked for the revolutionary front and were murdered by someone opposing the front.[26] Reagan's human rights commissioner, Ernest Lefever, declared that priests and nuns were engaged in activities against the government. He made a bizarre statement about "nuns hiding guns beneath their habits." And even more outrageously, Secretary of State Alexander Haig testified before the House Foreign Affairs Committee that perhaps the vehicle the nuns were riding in had tried to run a roadblock, and also that there may have been an exchange of fire. It was clear that the American government had made up its mind to discredit the missionaries, even if it meant flying in the face of all the evidence and portraying them as gun-toting nuns engaged in a shoot-out with the military at a roadblock. (The FBI said early on that there were no bullet holes in the van and that the women had been killed execution style.) Imagine the outrage of the loved ones of these nuns, who knew them to be deeply spiritual ministers to the poor, having to watch them be discredited by their own government.

Despite promises of an investigation by the Salvadoran government, little was done. In May this travesty was exposed by White, who revealed the cover-up once more, as well as the fact that the government was holding six national guardsmen for the crime and had known of their guilt from the beginning. White also believed that direct orders from officers had been given for the slaying.[27] Bill Ford wanted to know the names of the arrested men and wrote Congress of his conviction that these underlings were ordered to kill the women by someone higher in command.

Robert White was relieved of his position by Deane Hinton, but the new ambassador continued to press for justice. Bill Ford was received graciously by Salvadoran President Jose Duarte, who said his hands were tied since it was not a military crime for a soldier to kill a civilian! However, the constant pressure of the families and strong protest back in the United States from religious groups began to bring results. Congress voted to require Reagan to condition economic assistance on the honoring of human rights in El Salvador. Mention of the murder of the four women was included in the bill.

Threatened with loss of economic support, the Salvadoran government decided to put the six guardsmen on trial. But the trial was regularly postponed, until finally one of the guardsmen was "missing in action" and another was killed "on active duty." It became clear that neither the military nor the government wanted to proceed with the trial, probably because it would have incriminated the higher officers. Several years later, a former Salvadoran officer told Walter Cronkite on the *CBS Evening News* that it was Colonel Edgardo Casanova who had issued the order to kill the women. Many had suspected Casanova for some time. The former officer also said that the cover-up went all the way to the top of the government. In a later interview, this same informant indicated that the women were killed because they were subversives. Ita and Maura were listed as couriers to the guerrillas and Jean and Dorothy were condemned for their contacts with revolutionaries. He reiterated that it was Colonel Casanova who issued the order to kill the women. It was clear that no guardsman would take it upon himself to kill Americans without orders from above.

The bloody conflict in El Salvador ended in 1992. It cost 75,000 Salvadorans their lives and the United States spent seven billion dollars in aid. In 1984, four guardsmen were convicted of killing the women and were sentenced to thirty years in jail. Bill Ford pursued the case against Generals Garcia and Vides Casanova (cousin of Colonel Edgardo Casanova), who were the commanders at that time. In 2000 a Federal jury shocked the families by clearing the two generals on the grounds that they could not have stopped the crime. Both are now living comfortably as residents of Florida. In 2002, Bill Ford and the families won a $54.6 million liability suit against the two generals for torturing two Salvadorans.[28] Bill Ford died in 2008.

Jean's friend Father Crowley offered this reflection:

> There was no one, I would say, for whom life was more sweet than Jean Donovan. She was a totally human person. She lived life to the hilt.... And when she was asked to play her hand of cards her way—to say something that she personally was convinced of for the poor of South America, she did it in her own unique way.[29]

chapter two

Sister Helen Prejean, C.S.J.

"Time to go," said the warden. The condemned man, Patrick Sonnier, moved toward the room where he was to be executed, his chains scraping along the floor. Sister Helen, who had walked with him for years anticipating this event, was allowed to put her hand on his shoulder for the first time. She accompanied him to the oak electric chair, kissed him on the back, and then moved out to the witness room.

Patrick publicly asked for forgiveness for what he had done, and was strapped to the chair. He found Helen's face and said: "I love you," and Helen stretched her hand toward him and said: "I love you, too." Electrodes were connected to Patrick's head and leg, a switch was pulled several times, and soon after, the prisoner was pronounced dead. Helen left the prison in the dark and cold, was met by some of her sisters and friends, and began the long ride home. She reflected: "...I love this man, this spark of God, who has taught me so much"[1] As they drove down the highway Helen asked the driver to pull over; she got out and vomited. This was the end of Helen's years of struggle to save Patrick's life, of countless visits with him as he awaited his death. It was the beginning of an ongoing commitment to condemned prisoners, to the families of their victims, and to advocacy against capital punishment.

Early Life

Helen Prejean was born in 1939 in Baton Rouge, Louisiana. Her parents lived comfortably in a large home and were devoted to their three children. Her father, Louis, a lawyer, taught Helen to love books and to enjoy a good argument. Her mother, Gusta Mai, a nurse, passed on her gift of compassion to her daughter. Both parents, according to Helen, loved their children immensely.[2]

The family was well-off enough to have servants, who lived in a small house out back. Helen grew up in the South of the forties and fifties, a time when blacks could not attend white schools, had to sit at the back of the bus and in the side pews of the church, and receive Communion after the white folk. As a young girl, Helen was fascinated with what she saw as the vibrancy and spontaneity in people of color, but she was discouraged from associating with them. On one occasion she was shocked to see a young black woman literally kicked off a bus onto the pavement. Her father often represented black clients for a minimal charge, but neither he nor his wife seemed to question the racial discrimination of the time.

The family was Catholic of the '50s vintage, reciting the daily rosary, watching Bishop Sheen on TV, regularly hosting priests at home, and hoping that at least one of the children would have a vocation. Helen attended Catholic school and was taught by the Sisters of St. Joseph of Medaille, whom she found to be warm, loving, and "funny." Helen loved the Mass with its awesome sense of mystery. She says, "It gave me a sense of this invisible presence—that God was somehow with me and the most important thing was to do God's will, to hear that voice and follow it."[3]

After high school, Helen decided that rather than getting married and starting her own little family, she would "go wide" and become a "bride of Christ."[4] She believed that it was God's will that she join the sisters that had taught her, so she packed her black and white clothes and a pair of "old lady shoes," and was driven to a convent in New Orleans, crying all the way.

The Sisters of St. Joseph had been founded in the seventeenth century by four Frenchwomen who wanted to care for homeless children. The sisters Helen encountered were like many nuns of the time, women who dressed in full-flowing habits, led sheltered, semi-cloistered lives, and had few educational opportunities.

By the time Helen entered the community in 1957, it was beginning to change. In 1950 Rome had instructed sisters to gain better educational and theological training and to better accommodate modernity. Then Vatican II encouraged radical church renewal. The Council urged sisters to rediscover the original vision of their congregations, and to play an active role in the church in the modern world.

Members of Helen's community moved away from the hierarchical structures in community and adopted more modern lifestyles. They also took on a variety of new ministries, especially those concerned with serving the poor and advocating for social justice.

At first, Helen was slow adapting to this change. After all, she thought she had joined the convent to be a nun, not a social worker! In graduate school she enjoyed the freedom of going to pizza parties, playing her guitar, and becoming friends with priests, but it took some sorting out for her. Many sisters were leaving and she had to ask herself whether she wanted to join them. She was more drawn to the spiritual than to activism and social justice, so she was inclined to stay on the sidelines of this renewal, teaching her classes and then hurrying back to the cloister.

It wasn't until 1980, during a retreat given by Sister Marie Augusta Neal, a PH.D. from Harvard and a major figure in leading American sisters to the service of justice, that Helen's perspective began to change. Helen recalls how Neal started with an overview of the plight of the poor in the world. Helen knew that already. But then Sister Marie Augusta talked about Jesus' preaching to the poor. Helen thought she knew what would come next—the poor would be with God in heaven. But Marie Augusta did not say that. Instead she said that Jesus' good news was that the poor should be poor no longer! She was being called not to just pray for the poor and leave it to God to take care of them, but to take action to help raise people out of poverty.[5]

The next year Helen put her belongings in a pickup truck and drove from her comfortable convent to a noisy and chaotic housing project. She was told to put her bed below window level, where it would be safer from random gunfire. Through the long, lonely nights she would read the lives of her new heroes: Gandhi, Martin Luther King, Jr., and Dorothy Day. During the day she would work at an adult learning center, teaching the locals reading.

It was as though Helen had traveled to a different galaxy. Here she found adults who had graduated from public schools but were illiterate, as well as young dropouts, drug dealers, addicts, teenaged girls who clutched their infants, and grief stricken mothers of gunned-down teens. These now were *her* people. She spent her days helping single mothers make ends meet or counseling teens away from peddling drugs. Helen, who had spent so many hours in prayer, began to learn that prayer and action can become one. She writes: "Before, I had asked God to right the wrongs and comfort the suffering. Now I know—really know—that God entrusts those tasks to us."[6]

A New Beginning

One evening in 1982, Helen was asked if she would be a pen pal to someone on death row. Thinking that this would be just part of her new work with the poor, Helen agreed. She wrote her first letter to Patrick Sonnier, and enclosed some pictures, including one of herself and one of Jesus on the cross. Helen was surprised when Patrick answered and said that her letter was welcome. They began to correspond regularly.

Patrick would tell her about his day; he spent twenty-three hours in a six-by-eight cell, outfitted with a bunk, a toilet, and a wash basin. His one hour out could be spent with the eleven others on his tier, but relations were often tense or worse. His mother was ill, so she seldom visited, and his brother was in the same prison serving a life sentence.

Investigating the Crime

After several months, Helen became curious about Patrick's crime. She was allowed to examine the files and discovered that Patrick and his brother, Eddie, were convicted of attacking a teenaged girl and her boyfriend on a lovers' lane, raping the girl and shooting them both in the back of the head. The two killers were identified by other couples whom they had similarly molested but had survived their attacks. Eddie was given a life sentence, but Patrick was sentenced to death. The gruesome details of the murders and thoughts of what the victims' parents must have gone through nearly overwhelmed Helen. Even though she abhorred the evil Patrick had done, she was drawn by his loneliness, his abandonment, and need for care. She writes: "But I sense something, some sheer and essential humanness, and that, perhaps, is what draws me most of all."[7]

Spiritual Director

Helen next asked Patrick how she might go about visiting him and he answered that he would like her to be his spiritual advisor. She applied for the position, and was interviewed by an aging chaplain who warned her that these men were "the scum of the earth" and couldn't be trusted. He told her to wear her habit at all times and just prepare the convicts for the sacraments. Disconcerted by the advice, she gained approval and in September went for her first visit to Patrick.

Helen was surprised when she saw him: a handsome, clean-cut young man in immaculate clothes. He was bright and talkative, filling her in on the details of his early life on welfare, his failed marriage, and his other stint in jail. He never mentioned the crime. Looking back, she remembers her naïveté at the time—of not realizing that she had to also give attention to the victims' families and being surprised that those who faced execution did not have adequate legal defense.

The following year Patrick received word that the date had been set for his execution. He began to lose his appetite and his weight dropped quickly. An appeal was in the works and, while waiting, Helen discovered that Patrick's brother was actually the trigger man in the crime. She also discovered from a lawyer friend that the jury selection for the trial was flawed and that Patrick had had a weak defense lawyer. She was beginning to get the picture: A lot of death row inmates are poor and get defended poorly.[8] In addition, Patrick was tried in the South, in what is commonly referred to as the Death Belt—Louisiana, Georgia, Texas, and Florida—where two-thirds of all United States executions are carried out.

Helen decided to take part in the appeal process and she got Bishop Stanley Joseph Ott of Baton Rouge and some lawyers to visit the governor's office. The governor listened to their appeal, but felt that he was carrying out the will of the people in going through with the execution. Helen discovered that this was how most of the officials distanced themselves from the killing. They were "just doing their jobs."

It's Nothing Personal
Helen came to realize that in the prison system there was nearly always a disconnect between personal values and the public duty to be carried out. The arbitrariness and randomness of the sentencing of the poor, the psychological torture of those who waited years before execution, and the fact that executions did not deter crime, all seemed to be set aside in the name of following orders. People could consider themselves deeply religious and at the same time carry out executions. Additionally, Helen realized there was no individual responsibility for these executions. The name of the executioner was always kept secret and he was paid per execution by verbal agreement, with no paperwork. One guard even whispered in the ear of a condemned man before the switch was pulled something to the effect that it was nothing personal.[9] To render the whole process more "civilized," a white tablecloth dinner was served to the prisoner the night before, attended by the warden, lawyers, and guards who wanted to come. They all held hands and sang hymns together. And the next day the prisoner was killed!

The End Approaches
Helen and her lawyer friend made one late appeal to the Pardon Board, but to no avail. At the meeting, Helen was confronted by the victims'

families and regretted that she had neglected to minister to them as well. Helen began to plan Patrick's funeral Mass and visited the death house to make plans for a prayer service for him. Suddenly, while there, Helen caused some commotion by fainting. (Apparently she had been working hard on an empty stomach and no food was available to her in the prison.)

A communion service was eventually conducted and Patrick's mood seemed to lighten. He thanked Helen for loving him and she left, still hoping for a last minute stay of execution, which was denied. On the next visit, Patrick dropped to one knee and said: "Sister Helen, I'm going to die." Helen wrote about that moment:

> My soul rushes toward him. I am standing with my hands against the mesh screen, as close as I can get to him. I pray and ask God to comfort him, cushion him, wrap him around, give him courage to face death, to step across the river, to die with love. The words are pouring out of me.[10]

She thought of Gandhi and his commitment to nonviolence and of Camus's observation that for five centuries Christians believed that Jesus forbade killing.

Patrick's hair was shaved so that it wouldn't catch fire. He wrote his last will and testament, and when he was finished began to shiver. He turned down the last rites because he didn't like the priest and told Helen to receive Communion for both of them. Patrick was taken to the electric chair and then electrocuted.

The Aftermath

When Helen returned home, she was given a sleeping pill and fell into a deep, restful sleep. Several days later Bishop Ott offered the funeral Mass and Patrick was buried in a special cemetery alongside priests and nuns. A reporter asked her if she was in love with Patrick, because of his last words, "I love you." She smiled at the thought of the possible sensational headline in *The National Enquirer*: "Nun falls in love with murderer," and answered: "I loved Pat as a sister loves a brother, as Jesus taught us to love each other; it was not a romantic relationship."[11]

When it was all over, Helen decided she was through being pen pals or visiting anyone on death row! But she still had to face the outrage in the press, that Patrick had been given a hero's farewell Mass by a bishop and buried with priests and nuns. It was reported that a naïve and misguided nun had given her support to a murderer who should burn in hell.

Helen returned to her former work, but still kept an interest in support for victims' families, adequate legal representation for the poor, and the training of spiritual advisors for those on death row. On her annual retreat, she rested, prayed, and reflected on how the poor and powerless are the ones executed. After her retreat, she attended a meeting concerned about abolishing the death penalty and made an important decision: She would devote herself to speaking out against capital punishment.

Robert Lee Willie
When Helen was asked to be spiritual advisor for another young man on death row, she was at first reluctant but then allowed herself to be persuaded. She would walk with a new prisoner, Robert Lee Willie. Willie had a long history of crime, including murders, rapes, robberies, and drug dealing. He was on death row for raping and murdering an eighteen-year-old woman.

Helen was warned that she would encounter opposition. Two Catholic priest chaplains had told the warden that Helen was naïve, had been emotionally involved with Sonnier, and had caused trouble with her fainting episode. They charged that Helen was also blind to the fact that Sonnier may have lost his soul by refusing last rites. In general, the chaplains maintained that women were just too emotional for this kind of work.

To defend herself, Helen went to see the warden. Helen knew that prisoners had a constitutional right to have a spiritual advisor of their choice and she wanted to present her case for acting in that role. After a lively discussion with the warden about capital punishment, she clarified her sisterly relationship with Patrick and explained how hunger had caused the fainting incident. Finally, she said that she firmly believed that love was Patrick's sacrament and that he died at peace with Jesus. The warden was impressed and approved Helen to be Willie's spiritual advisor.

Visiting Willie

Helen started visiting Willie and the two began getting acquainted. Meanwhile, she encountered the mother and stepfather of Willie's victim, Faith Harvey. They invited Helen to come to visit them. They told her the whole gruesome story of the murder of their beloved daughter. All the while, they assumed that Helen was completely supportive of Willie's execution, even though she informed them that she was his spiritual advisor. The friendship with the couple would be short-lived, when Helen attempted to get a stay of execution at the meeting of the pardon board a month later. Even though Helen deeply shared their grief and understood their need for retribution, she could not take part in their hatred of Willie or in their desire to see him killed.

Helen's mission with Willie was different from the one she had with Sonnier. To Patrick she offered tenderness and love and helped restore his human dignity. With Robert, she was more confrontational. He was unrepentant for his crimes, filled with racial hatred; he was an admirer of Hitler and had earlier joined the Aryan Brotherhood, a white-supremacist group. Her goal was to challenge him to take responsibility for his crime and to ask forgiveness of his victim's family. She wanted to see him die with dignity and integrity.[12] Meanwhile, Helen and her lawyer friends worked to question the legality of Willie's trial. Despite pleas from both Willie and Helen to the pardon board, Willie was perceived as unrepentant, blaming his problems on politicians, and was declared to be still deserving of execution. The Harveys were shocked at Helen's defense of Willie to the board and wrote her off as someone who had betrayed them.

Willie Repents

Finally, Willie was repentant and apologized to the Harveys.[13] He asked Helen to be with him right to the end. She succeeded in convincing

Willie to admit that all his talk about Hitler and wanting to be a terrorist was stupid. At the same time, he said he wanted to die as a tough outlaw and proud of it. Helen urged him to die with love in his heart.

After a friendly visit with his family, Willie enjoyed his last meal, pleased now that he was "going to a better place." Softening, he cried during a last telephone conversation with his family. He thanked Helen for not being a "preachy" nun, but rather a nice friend with whom he could freely talk. In his last words, he told his victim's parents that he hoped his death would offer them some relief. Nevertheless he believed that killing, including executions, were always wrong. Willie had learned well from his mentor, Helen, and as he was strapped into the chair he found her face and gave her a wink. Willie wanted to be "cool" to the very end.

Helen's Case Against Capital Punishment

In her writings, Helen Prejean shares the insights she has gained with regard to capital punishment over the years. Helen maintains that there are two main reasons why people support the death penalty: 1. They are scared of crime and violence and believe that executions will somehow make them safer, and, 2. The death penalty is removed from them, in that executions are statistics and they never see anyone executed. She firmly believes that through education people can be brought to no longer support the death penalty. For instance, she cites polls that reveal that when people understand the alternative of life imprisonment without parole, their support of execution drops below fifty percent.[14] When statistics demonstrate that the death penalty does not deter crime, support for execution drops significantly. She quotes the famous Supreme Court Justice Thurgood Marshall, who wrote about public opinion on the death penalty: "If they were better informed they would consider it shocking, unjust and unacceptable."[15] Helen thinks that such education is not sufficiently taking place today, and that many people are still of the opinion that the death penalty will deter crime and keep them safe.

Helen's Mission

Helen has now long been a student of the death penalty and has traveled extensively educating people to oppose it. Helen points to the racial factor in executions. She observes that in her home state of Louisiana blacks are seldom executed for killing blacks. Although the majority of homicide victims there are black, the majority of death-row inmates are there for killing whites. She notes that all-white juries are still commonplace in many areas of the South. She cites some other alarming statistics. In Alabama, 31 percent of the black population has been incarcerated and accounts for 70 percent of executions. Nationally, though blacks account for only 12 percent of the population, they account for over 40 percent of those who are given the death penalty.[16]

In addition, 99 percent of those on death row are poor, and have public defenders who scarcely have time to interview them or do the time-consuming investigation needed for capital cases.[17]

Sister Helen is encouraged by the fact that most states have revised their criminal codes to require life without parole for aggravated or capital murder, and that many states have extended the time to be served before the prisoner can be eligible for parole. Helen is also pleased that more states realize the extreme cost of executions, and what a serious diversion of funds away from crime-fighting programs this can be. Texas, which has more than three hundred persons on death row, spends $2.3 million on each capital case, and yet its murder rate is one of the highest in the country. In contrast, New York City, which is in a state where there is no death penalty, has been able to cut its crime rate substantially by tripling its police force.[18]

The Constitution and the Death Penalty

Helen Prejean insists that the death penalty is unconstitutional. She points out that the Supreme Court decisions on the death penalty in fact bypass the cruelty issue. In the famous case *Furman v. Georgia* in 1972 the court found the death penalty to be unconstitutional, not because it was cruel, but because it was too arbitrary and capricious in its implementation. The court pointed out that juries, lacking specific guidance, frequently imposed the death penalty based on race or randomness. In response to *Furman*, state legislatures redrafted their capital statutes so that the death penalty would be imposed more fairly. Then in 1976 in *Gregg* v. *Georgia*, the court ruled that Georgia's new capital laws removed the randomness and capriciousness from capital punishment and made assurances that the death penalty would be imposed more even-handedly.

The court decided that the death penalty did not violate the Eighth Amendment's prohibition of cruel and unusual punishment because it was accepted by the framers and had a long history of approval in this country. The court pointed out that a large percentage of Americans consider the death penalty appropriate and necessary, and an expression of outrage for serious crimes, and thus hold it just. The court seems to ignore the many studies that show that the death penalty is not a deterrent of crime.[19] As a result of the views of the court, other states followed Georgia's new statute reform and reinstated the death penalty.

Chief Justice Antonin Scalia

Ironically, Chief Justice Scalia, whom Helen views as one of the justices who authorize executions and as a self-proclaimed "part of the machinery of death," is close friends with Helen's brother, Louie. In a chance meeting with the justice in an airport, Helen had a vigorous discussion with him about the death penalty. She learned that Scalia is a literalist and gives little attention to the modern context. He focuses on what he believes to be the understanding of the Constitution at the time it was adopted. For him the Constitution is not a living document that allows for new interpretations, but a document frozen in time. Since the framers forbade cruel punishment and yet sanctioned the death penalty, he holds that they did not consider it to be cruel. No matter that they wrote the Constitution in a different context, one in which the death penalty was allowed for rape, horse stealing, arson, and even witchcraft. No matter that the framers insisted on due process, equal justice, fair trials, impartial juries, and adequate defenses. Helen maintains that many of these factors are lacking in today's capital cases. In their conversation, Justice Scalia admitted that today's context is of little importance. He said that he takes his best shot at getting the fairest meaning of the text at the time it was adopted.[20]

This ignoring of today's context, according to Helen, has led Scalia to dissent when the court declared it unconstitutional to execute the mentally handicapped. For him, the understanding of the Constitution cannot evolve to accommodate modern insights and new situations. Helen vehemently disagrees, pointing out how the court erroneously allowed the infamous Jim Crow laws and the suppression of civil and educational rights for blacks in this country. Helen is blunt in her views on the legality of the death penalty:

> I reject the constitutionality of the death penalty because I have seen close up how the death penalty operates. The Supreme Court could declare the death penalty unconstitutional tomorrow morning if it were willing to confront the unfair patterns that have emerged in the last twenty-five years of state killing.[21]

She believes that the framers of the Constitution would be appalled by the way constitutional protections of defendants have been ignored or abused in the administration of the death penalty. Helen is convinced that the framers would also be moved by how many of our international allies have abandoned the death penalty over the last fifty years. During this period, over eighty countries of the world have abolished the death penalty.[22]

Helen vehemently opposes Scalia's position on the death penalty. She agrees with the position of former Justice Harry Blackmun who considered the death penalty to be indeed the "cruel and unusual punishment," forbidden by the Eighth Amendment. And Helen shares Blackmun's view that death in the electric chair is a throwback to more primitive times, when people were burned at the stake.[23]

Church Teaching

Helen has a difficult time seeing how Christians can follow Jesus, who taught forgiveness and that his disciples should not return hate for hate or evil for evil, and yet at the same time support execution. She wonders how Christians could have accommodated his mandate for compassion and nonviolence to end lives with the death penalty. Helen realizes that the "vengeful God" of the Old Testament is often used to justify executions, but she is repelled by this notion of a God filled with rage and bent on retaliation.

Helen points out that for three centuries Christians were committed to nonviolence. Then once the church was embraced by the Roman Empire, it began to take on the imperial ways of violence. The acceptance of violence was then given a theology by Augustine, who developed the "just war" theory and legitimized violence against wicked enemies. Since then the history of Christianity has been replete with violence, wars, and executions.[24]

Helen's experience on death row has led her to reject this acceptance of violence, especially with regard to those on death row. She believes that any group of people can't be trusted to decide on the punishment of death. Moreover, Helen is appalled that so many Christians, and Catholics more than Protestants, support the death penalty. She supports the American bishops' statement that the death penalty is unfair and discriminatory, a practice that disregards human dignity. However, Helen disagrees with their position that the state has the right to kill individuals.

Sister Helen was pleased when, in 1995, John Paul II spoke out against the death penalty, even though he still supported the state's right to execute in cases of "absolute necessity." She wrote a letter to the pope and shared her experience with him, pointing out how strong the race element was in executions in the United States. She believes that her letter, along with much work by national bishops' conferences resulted in the pope's ordering the *Catechism of the Catholic Church* to be changed so

that capital punishment was to be allowed "very rarely." Pope John Paul
II became more adamant in his own teaching against the death penalty.[25]
It is Helen's hope that Justice Scalia who considers himself to be a traditional Catholic, will give more consideration to the church's official
teaching against capital punishment.[26]

The Killing of the Innocents
Helen's rejection of the death penalty was compounded by her experience with the execution of innocent people. Her book *The Death of
Innocents* tells the story of her ministry to two such men who were put
to death. The first was Dobie Gillis Williams, an indigent black man
with an IQ of sixty-five, and a frail body wracked with rheumatoid
arthritis. Helen visited Dobie for eight years, through many tortuous
last-minute stays and prolonged efforts to show how flimsy the evidence
was against him. She often assured Dobie that he was a good human
being and that Jesus was close to him, giving him the strength he
needed. He was heartened by the prayers of Trappists, convents of sisters, and even a community in Rome.

Though many state and federal courts have been forced to free
wrongly convicted people from death row, Dobie did not receive such
justice. He was quickly convicted by an all-white jury of killing a white
woman, even though there was no real evidence that he had committed
the crime. He died forgiving his persecutors and blessing everyone in
the room.

The other death row victim whom Helen accompanied was Joseph
O'Dell, a white man, a veteran of prisons, accused of raping and murdering a secretary. The blood, semen, and hair evidence were "consistent" with O'Dell but there was no proof that he had committed the
crime. He was convicted on the testimony of a jailhouse informant.
Helen worked hard with others throughout the world to exonerate
O'Dell and even enlisted the help of John Paul II, Mother Teresa, a member of the Italian Parliament, and thousands of Italians who were active
anti–death penalty advocates to intercede for him to the governor of

Virginia. All appeals were denied, even the one in which new DNA tests could have proved O'Dell innocent.

Joseph was strapped to a gurney and executed by injection. Amazingly, the Italian Parliament, which worked tirelessly to bring attention to this case as well as the death penalty throughout the world, paid to have Joseph's body shipped to Palermo and buried with dignity. While in Italy for the funeral, Helen visited the pope who shared with her that he had prayed for Joseph. The jailhouse informant (who testified against O'Dell) later wrote to Helen, admitting he had lied in order to get released.

A Call to Join In

Sister Helen Prejean has become a leading advocate against the death penalty. She has accompanied many men to their deaths, given countless talks across the country, and ministered to families of victims. She encourages all of us to join her in her mission: "I invite you to join me in the struggle to end the death penalty in the United States and around the world. Its practice demeans us all. See you on the road."[27]

chapter three

Sister Dorothy Stang, S.N.D. DE N.

"Call the nun!" was the unexpected advice that the two young men received when they arrived in Brazil in 2003 to do a documentary on the rainforests. They were given a confidential phone number by Greenpeace and, with some difficulty, were able to contact a Sister Dorothy, who had been active for many years in and around the jungle town of Anapu in the northwest of Brazil. After a five-minute crackling conversation, they were so taken with her that they decided to travel twenty-five hundred miles and try to meet her in a remote area of the jungle, east of the Amazon in the state of Para.

The two adventurers, James Newton and Sam Clements, set out on the long journey, first by plane, then by crowded boat, and finally over dusty roads by bus. They endured intense heat, felt the constant onslaught of insects, and had to check their shoes each morning for tarantulas, scorpions, and other insects. While on the Amazon, the largest river in the world, they were amazed at the beauty surrounding them.

As they approached Anapu, they soon learned from the many stories about "Irma Dorothy," the seventy-two-year-old nun who was legendary in the area for her work with the poor and her efforts to preserve the rain forest. They also heard that her life was in danger.

Eventually, Sam and Jim were taken to a building to meet Dorothy. They expected an old, frail lady, but instead a vivacious woman burst forth to hug them and give them a lovely rose. The unlikely threesome set off by boat, and upon landing on shore, Dorothy drove her Jeep to show them the magnificent rainforest, which in so many places had been destroyed by illegal ranchers and loggers. The two young men were quickly taken with the energy, enthusiasm, and humor of this nun. They met many of the poor locals who had become sister's community and they passed the many graves of those who had been murdered by the hired guns of the ranchers and loggers for protesting the injustices.

When the time came for the two to leave, they embraced their new friend and she said to them: "Keep rowing upstream, Sam and James." They left her standing on the shore smiling, looking both courageous and so vulnerable. They were worried about Dorothy's safety, and their concerns were justified. Two years later and soon after returning to England, they heard that Dorothy had been shot dead by two assassins. They dedicated their documentary to their beloved friend.[1]

Early Years
"Dot," as everyone called her, was born in 1931, the middle child of nine children, and raised near Dayton, Ohio. Her father, Henry, was an officer at a nearby air base and was trained as a chemical engineer. He also ran a small organic farm, where he taught his children how chemicals damage the soil and showed them how to make compost out of all the family's leftovers. Dot's mother, Edna, was a traditional homemaker and devoted mother, who worked hard raising her large family and maintaining the household.[2]

Dorothy grew up in the hard times of the Depression and was taught to not waste and to share with poor neighbors. She and her eight siblings lived simply and worked extra jobs to bring in money for the family. She also grew up during a time in which the Catholic faith was central to family life—from daily Masses, weekly confessions, and family rosaries to the many statues and sacramentals well-placed throughout the home. Catholic education was the rule, not the exception. From the beginning, Dorothy's Catholicism played a pivotal role in her life and choices.

A Vocation

When Dot was young, those around her recognized that she might have a vocation. Back then, most Catholic families expected that one or more of their children would enter the seminary or convent.[3]

Dorothy's vocation was nurtured in her family and schools. In grade school she gained interest in the missions and joined in the fundraising to save "pagan babies." In high school Dorothy became a leader in the Young Christian Student movement and learned the power of small enthusiastic groups.[4] From the Notre Dame Sisters who taught her, she learned the value of education and took on the ideal of serving the poorest of the poor from the order's founder, Saint Julie Billiart.[5]

Becoming a Sister

Before finishing high school, Dot decided to join the Notre Dame sisters, hoping to become a missionary and serve the poor. When Dot entered the convent, religious sisters wore elaborate habits, were quite strict in their rules, and spent much time in prayer, work, and study. They were separated from their families and the world, and received rigorous discipline to enable them to keep their vows of poverty, chastity, and obedience. Dot (now Sister Mary Joachim) took on the new life with a passion, made her vows and was given her first "mission" in 1951 at age twenty.

Mission

Dot's initial mission hardly matched her calling. Instead of being sent to some faraway country to serve the poor and save pagans, she was assigned to teach children in St. Victor School in Calumet City, Illinois. The next year she was transferred to another school, and the following year she volunteered for a mission with a new school in Arizona. Many of Dot's former students still remember her as a loving and caring woman who gave many of her students personal guidance.[6]

Among Migrant Workers

A key part of Dot's Arizona experience was the opportunity she had to work with migrant workers on Friday afternoons. Once she saw their extreme poverty, she knew she was now moving closer to her real "mission"—working with the poorest of the poor.

Dot began to learn Spanish and joined the migrants in the fields as they bent over for long hours picking crops in the scorching sun, some mothers dragging their babies behind them in cardboard boxes. She urged the workers to get an education for their children, to avoid the chemicals from the crop-dusting planes, and to organize themselves into unions. During that same period, Cesar Chavez was organizing migrant workers, and the spirit of his movement influenced Dot in her own work.[7]

A Foreign Mission at Last

Dot was thirty-five when she finally had the opportunity to volunteer for the kind of mission she always longed for—a chance to serve the poor in far-off Brazil. In August of 1966 she arrived in Petropolis, Brazil, and began to study at a center there, taking demanding courses in the native Portuguese language, as well as Brazilian history, politics, religion, and local customs.

This was the '60s, a time of enormous political and cultural shifts. Dot broke out of her religious bubble and was introduced to missionaries from all over the world.

She climbed mountains with French "worker priests," who shed their clerical garb for overalls and stood side by side with factory workers. She met priests, nuns, and laypeople who had become radicalized by the progressive teachings of Vatican II. She studied under professors who espoused the new and controversial liberation theology, and experienced the power of base communities, where the Gospels were linked to action for justice and freedom.[8]

The Vatican II Perspective

Dot was excited by the teachings of the Second Vatican Council. She learned that the church was first and foremost the "people of God," and she wanted to be part of this "new church" and teach all people, especially God's poor, the message of love, compassion, and justice. Dot no longer wanted to leave the world, but to be in the world to bring it the gospel message of love and justice. She decided that she would live in solidarity with the oppressed. She traded her elaborate habit for a simple skirt and blouse and prepared for her mission.[9]

Pastoral Work Among the Poor
Dot was assigned to a remote area of the world, Coroata, Brazil, a small town of forest peasants, most of whom were poor, hungry and often sick with malaria, worms, and tropical fevers. These peasants were caught in an age-old feudal system wherein they slaved for the few wealthy families who owned all the land in the area. If the peasants objected to the many abuses inflicted on them, they were threatened and even killed by gunmen, who were seldom punished. These peasants would be Dot's "people of God" and she and three other sisters settled in to serve them from their first "house," a half caved-in structure filled with rodents and bats.

The sisters were assigned to do pastoral work with thousands of peasants who had been trained in a rudimentary and superstitious version of Christianity. The sisters joined several dedicated priests and traveled around teaching the Gospels, picking out leaders, and organizing base communities to meet, pray, study, and discuss human rights. Such activity, of course, immediately alarmed the landowners, who saw the pastoral teams as "troublemakers," even communists, challenging their system.

The sisters knew that this struggle for justice and freedom would be a dangerous one. Walking with the poor, helping them understand their rights, and standing up to oppressors would bring them the label of "subversives" and "revolutionaries." The powerful and the wealthy had the political and military power, and the hired guns to intimidate and even eliminate those making such challenges.[10]

By 1974 Dot thought it was time to move farther into the interior, where thousands were settling along the new Transamazon Highway.

Dot's community warned her that she was already in danger and would now be going where many were being killed over property.

Reluctantly they allowed Dot and another sister to push deeper into the forest.

In the Midst of Land Disputes

There were many land disputes where Dot decided to work. The government received large loans from the World Bank, the United States, and other organizations to develop the Amazon region for ranching, logging, and mining. The government parceled out huge tracts to the wealthy and offered small farms to the poor. The deeds were often open to dispute. Those with the money and the guns usually won.

New highways and development drew multitudes. Some peasants came to work for the wealthy landowners, logging and planting grass for cattle. Once the work was done, these peasants were fired and had to search for scraps of land in the forest, where they were joined by the indigenous who had been driven off their ancestral lands. Small farmers would often homestead on land that was once theirs, but had been confiscated by the state. Once development came, the rich would return, often with illegal deeds, and armed with the firepower to drive the small farmers off the land.

This was the explosive situation that Dot and a member of her pastoral team Becky found themselves in when they arrived in an area called Abel Figueiredo and joined a Father Hoss in his ministry in 1974. Dot wrote that they had hardly started building base communities when the "land sharks" showed up, bloodied the peasants and burned their homes, while the police stood by with machine guns. Many were driven into the forests, where they were hunted down by the military. The devastation of the land was overwhelming. Already forty million acres of Brazilian rain forest had been destroyed for ranching or farming.

The Mission Is Established

Dot and her pastoral team were shocked by the blatant injustice and began to collect maps, legal documents, and testimony to protect the small landowners. They were able to save the land of some small farmers by producing the legal deeds to their property. They also taught the people to read the Bible and linked the Scriptures to their plight, and organized base communities to pray and join in faith to struggle for spiritual and physical liberation. (Base communities are often viewed negatively as is the term "liberation theology" or radical left-leaning political doctrines. However, base communities have enjoyed the blessing of Latin American bishops for at least two decades, are made up of devout Catholic men and women who are deeply interested in a different kind of "liberation" in a personal and moral sense, not only the physical or political sense.)

The land disputes heated up: Some peasants were arrested for resisting the claims of wealthy landowners; a number of activist priests were deported. With the disappearance of the priests, Dot and Becky received permission to baptize, hold Communion and reconciliation services, and anoint the sick and the dying. This activity raised loud objections from some of the Brazilian clergy and hierarchy who, though not willing to come into this dangerous area, still believed that their turf was being taken over.

Moving on Alone
In 1977, another highway was opened after many peasants had slaved to clear the forests for the roadway, only to be cast aside when it was finished. These poor drifters were joined by hundreds of new settlers looking for land. Dot decided to follow the poorest and most vulnerable of these people deep into the forests, to minister to them and to teach them their rights and how to stand up for themselves.

Dot traveled great distances to organize dozens of base communities, build schools for the education of the poor, and train teachers. She often waited hours in the forest in order to hitch a ride on a truck to get to her destination. She insisted on living as her people did, eating the same food, and sharing in the same dangers. As she traveled about, she slept in lean-to chapels, in makeshift classrooms, or on the dirt floor of a hut of one of her people.

Periodically, Dot would return to the States to visit her family and her community and to raise money for her work. Family members also visited her from time to time to help with her many projects.

Dot often confronted the ranchers and loggers, pointing out to them how unchristian their activities were and lecturing them on their unjust treatment of "her people." Many of them grew to hate her and often they threatened her. The authorities often put warrants out for her arrest, but usually Dot was warned in time and would disappear into the forest for a while. Gradually, Dot saw the danger closing in on her.

Dot then decided to make another move; this time to help her people better sustain the forests. In 1982, at the age of fifty-one, Dorothy decided to ask the local bishop if she could work with the poorest of the poor in the large and remote area near Altamira.

She settled herself in a place called Nazare, where she lived in a mud hut. Dot worked hard to meet all the pastoral needs of her people, while praying and celebrating with them. She now was an expert in organizing associations and cooperatives. She secured many jobs for people, helped them with their land issues, and made plans for a fruit processing factory, which would allow the people to make money and at the same time stop their slash-and-burn farming. She organized basket weaving, mural painting, well-digging, rice-cleaning, and many other occupations so that the residents could self-sustain. Dot also worked with the women, who were considered to be inferior, especially if they were black or Indian women. She taught them that they had dignity and should insist on equality. She established a women's association, which focused on family health, alternative medicines, and proper diet. Many women in the area still remember today how deeply Sister Dorothy affected their lives.[11]

Dot often would act as a legal advocate for her people. She would show up in the city of Brasília at offices of the federal police and the attorney general. They might make her sit and wait while they tried to avoid her, but more often than not Dot would get her opportunity to expose the illegal loggers and land grabbers and challenge the authorities. At times she would go on hunger strikes outside government offices, or sleep on the sidewalk waiting for them to come to work in the morning.

Education was Dot's passion. She believed that raising the educational level of her people was essential to their freedom and independence. In one area she established twenty-three schools and trained scores of teachers.[12] All the while, the dangers from her enemies still followed and she was alarmed when in 1988 she heard of the much-publicized murder of Chico Mendes, a Brazilian who shared her vision and work for saving the rain forests.

By 1991 Dot was sixty years old and had spent twenty-five of them in Brazil. She was thankful "that I've been able to live, love, and be loved, and work with the Brazilian people...."[13] She was thankful that she had given them confidence in themselves, helped them be aware that God was present in their lives, and assisted in the birth of a more humane society. But Dot was ready for a break. She had contracted malaria ten times and was now down with a severe case of dengue fever. In November, Dot returned to the States for a six-month sabbatical.

Creation Spirituality
Sister Dot saw her sabbatical as an opportunity to go back to school, so she enrolled for a semester course on creation-centered spirituality at the University of the Most Holy Name in California. This experience was a turning point for Dot. She was able to take a break from social activism and focus on her intense awareness of the presence of the Mother God in nature and a renewed notion of what her church and ministry meant to her. Dot grew tremendously during this period, both intellectually and spiritually. She had so much she wanted to bring back to her people. The rain forests were a blessing—they were nature's cathedrals where the divine dwelled. She believed that the people

should see themselves connected to nature and to all living things, and realize their mission was to sustain, preserve, and revere their environment. She would teach them to love and care for their fellow human beings rather than kill and destroy them. She would teach her people, especially the women, to resist patriarchal structures of family, church, and government and to insist on their rights of freedom and equality.[14]

Return to Brazil

On her return to Brazil, Dot attended the Earth Summit in Rio de Janeiro. She was inspired by the hundreds of thousands of environmentalists from all over the globe at the gathering and was further fortified in her mission to care for the earth.

Dot was ready to go back to work in Nazare and spend the rest of her days with her people. She joined a new pastoral team and started once again moving through the forest, organizing, teaching, and supporting the poor. Dot now wore painted T-shirts with the slogan: "The Death of the Forest Is the Death of Us All."[15] She began to teach her people to plant new trees instead of cutting trees down.

Things were changing in Dot's region. Her area had become a new county, which brought more political power to the area and made federal funds for development available. At the same time, many more migrants were attracted to the area, and there was an intense struggle for control.

Dot's letters from this time show that she didn't return with her old energy and enthusiasm. She was feeling frustrated and her age was beginning to take its toll. At one point, she wrote a touching prayer: "God, my Lover—you that wooed my heart to follow You even to other lands to serve—don't abandon me. I trust that You are with me—strengthen me daily—I'm fragile. I need you."[16]

In order to be more at the center of things, Dot moved from the tiny settlement of Nazare to the city of Anapu, where she was able to live in a new wooden house with cement floors, running water, and a telephone. She looked forward to the construction of a new church and enjoyed a huge celebration, with more than two thousand people, for the ordination of three young priests who would work in the parish.

After the celebration, reality set in once again for Dot and her team. The sale of drugs began to expand, the forests continued to be destroyed for their valuable hardwoods, the ranchers continued to slash and burn, and the violence increased. A religious brother who ran a printing press and served the community as a mechanic was shot dead, mistaken for the local priest.

Dot continued to persevere with her mission to help her people to sustain the area's land and trees. She encouraged the women to gather medicinal plants and urged the men to plant mahogany and cedar trees. She was joined by three young agricultural technicians who showed the farmers new skills in raising food. By then Dot had organized sixty-two schools in the area.

The Final Struggle

Dot's final struggle began at the end of the '90s, when the government declared that an enormous dam was to be built in her area. This project attracted hordes of migrants into the area as well as many rich landowners, some with forged deeds that they used to drive off homesteaders.

Dot's plan to teach her people sustainability was given support in 1997 when she received a government grant of two large areas of land for land reform and conservation.

Her idea was that the settlers would use 20 percent of their land and keep the rest as forest reserve. They would farm their land properly and replant trees.

Dot had her work cut out for her in maintaining her projects for sustainability. The land battle that Dot had fought for so many years was on again, but now on a much larger scale and with much higher stakes. She exposed the fake deeds of some landowners, advocated for land ownership by her people, and reported the illegal logging and ranching. Dot called for fines to be enforced on those who broke the law.

Losing Ground and Slowing Down

The situation heated up even more for Dorothy in 2003. Dot called in the government to check the situation, wherein loggers were encroaching on her sustainable land projects. A team of military police arrived and found a clandestine landing strip amid the areas that had been logged, as well as many men using heavy machinery, unlicensed chainsaws, and firearms. Millions of cubic feet of lumber had been stacked by the river. The operation was shut down and the machinery towed away. [17] That month Dot learned that a gunman named Tufi had been hired to kill her and that she had the highest price on her head of anyone in the area.

Dot was losing ground even with her own people, many of whom had now turned to the government instead of her co-ops and associations, and often they were fighting among themselves. Not a few resisted her notions of sustainability and returned to the old slash-and-burn methods. The old energy that had filled the base communities and inspired the people toward liberation was on the wane. [18]

Dot herself was slowing down, at times feeling her age, and finding it more difficult to walk the long distances on jungle paths to locate her people. She became more aware of the danger and once remarked: "I know they want to kill me, but I will not go away." [19] At times she felt very afraid, but would then say that being an American and an old woman would protect her.

Time Off

In 2004 Dot took a much-needed break. She joined a pilgrimage to see the sights and home of the founder of her order, Saint Julie. Dot felt kindred to Julie when she saw the simple hut she had lived in and the small parish church where she prayed. Dorothy related to the stories of how Julie had walked many miles to teach the poor, and how she suffered death threats during the French Revolution.

Dorothy then returned to Ohio to see friends and family. During the visit she was pensive, private, in need of much prayer time. She confided to some in her community of sisters that there were some back in Brazil who wanted her dead. In spite of this, Dot was determined to return.

The Final Years

When Dot went back to Brazil, she visited Brasília to request protection for her people. In twenty years there had been over 700 murders in her county, and few of those responsible had been convicted. The government officials assured her that there would be more protection and enforcement of the law, but little ever came of their promises.

In the fall of 2004 several of Dot's farmers were attacked by hooded gunmen and their houses were ransacked. The next day when the thugs returned, the farmers were ready, and in the ensuing battle, one of the invaders was killed. Dot was out of town at the time, but was hauled into court and charged with starting an armed rebellion. After she told the judge about all the violence that had been done to her farmers, she was released. The confrontations continued and the landowners began to discuss openly how to get rid of Dorothy.[20]

Ironically, at the same time that Dot's enemies were plotting her demise, she began to receive a series of public awards: The Chico Mendes Medal, Honorary Citizen of Para, and Woman of the Year. She was even given Brazilian citizenship. The awards brought much attention to Dorothy and she was interviewed by major newspapers and TV stations. The notoriety made Dot's enemies all the more nervous, and rumors spread that the ranchers and loggers had held a secret meeting in a hotel in Altamira to discuss how to get rid of this woman, who was exposing their forged deeds and illegal activities.

A rancher known as Bida said he would put up the money ($25,000) to have Dorothy killed; a man called Tato was appointed to set up the hit. Tato hired two men, Raifran and Clodoaldo, to kill Dot, with Raifran to be the trigger man.[21] An attempt was made to kill Dorothy one night after a meeting, but that night she had slept on the floor and was not visible enough to get a shot at her from outside the hut.

The next morning Dot rose early and started up the path to the community center. At the top of the hill the two killers stepped out in front of her and blocked her way. Dot greeted them kindly and talked to them gently about the earth and how wrong it was to abuse the forests. One of her associates, who was just behind her, ducked behind a tree and witnessed what happened next.

Dorothy took her maps out of a shoulder bag, spread them out on the ground and began to calmly explain the boundaries of the sustainable areas, where her farmers had the right to live and work. At that moment, Raifran was about to shoot her, but his partner waved him off.

Raifran then asked Dot if she had a weapon. Dot answered that the only weapon she had was her Bible and she took it out and began reading him the beatitudes. The gunman again was ready to shoot, but was waved off once more. Dot calmly invited them to the meeting and then turned and walked on with a characteristic, "God bless you, my sons."[22] The assassin drew his pistol and this time got the nod. He called Dot and when she turned and held her bible to shield herself, he shot her in the stomach. Dot fell to the ground face down, moaning softly. Then Raifran emptied his gun into Sister Dorothy's body and head. It was pouring rain and Dorothy's blood flowed into the rich soil under a canopy of trees, the very trees she had labored so hard to protect.

Eventually, some locals came and took Dorothy's limp and soggy body and placed it in the back of a pick-up truck and drove her to the hospital in Anapu. Many in the city were shocked at the news of Dot's death, but others set off firecrackers and celebrated, taunting the farmers that this is what they had coming.

As word of the killing spread across Brazil and around the world, two thousand troops were flown in to secure the area and hunt for the murderers. Dot's body was flown to Belem so that there could be an autopsy and identification. When the body arrived, a crowd had gathered with banners demanding justice and shouting: "Dorothy, vive!" The sisters were inundated with calls from all over the world and many global organizations sent their condolences. After the autopsy, the sisters were able to have private time with the body, and they dressed her in her favorite dress with a sunflower pattern. They observed that Dot's face was peaceful and serene.

The body was taken to the local church, where Masses were offered. Dot was surrounded by bishops, priests, sisters, and many of her followers. Her body was flown back to her mission area, where more services were held. Dorothy's simple casket was then taken to the center where she worked, the place where she had asked to be buried. A procession of over two thousand people, including government and church officials and the many poor that Dorothy had served, accompanied the casket to the gravesite. One of the sister superiors remarked: "Today, we are not going to bury Dorothy; we are going to plant her." Everyone shouted: "Dorothy, vive!" Dot's body was placed in the simple grave.[23]

The Aftermath

Dorothy Stang's enemies had hoped that the commotion over her death would soon blow over, but instead her murder became a global event. International organizations pointed to her death and underlined the environmental destruction that was going on in Brazil. The government was denounced internationally for allowing the devastation of its rain forests, as well as for overlooking the many murders of the landless poor. Dorothy was held up by many as a martyr for the causes of the environment and the poor. Countless stories came forth from people that Dot had helped, rescued, taught, protected, and inspired.

The international attention given to Dorothy and her mission, as well as to the neglect of the government, had its impact. Just days after her killing, President Lula da Silva of Brazil, created two new national parks in the Amazon area and signed a decree to protect millions of acres of the rain forest. A large area called "Project Dorothy Stang" was set aside for the poor sustainable farmers.

In spite of these positive steps, land disputes and activist killings still continue. Foreign corporations and agribusinesses still struggle to control Amazonia. And yet, many still share the conviction expressed at Dot's grave by a woman trained by her: "Dorothy, we promise to continue using your smile and your faith every day in our struggle, and to continue planting seeds of love, peace, and social justice."[24]

Was Justice Served?

Just days after Dorothy's brutal killing, the U.S. State Department pushed for justice and sent FBI agents to help with the investigation. Raifran, the shooter, was tried, convicted of first degree murder, and sentenced to twenty-seven years in prison. Clodoaldo was given seventeen years for his part in the crime. Both testified that Tato offered to pay them for the shooting and named Bida (Vitalmiro Bastos de Moura) and Regivaldo Galvao as the ones who masterminded the killing. Tato was tried, convicted, and sentenced to eighteen years. Galvao was released, because the court had determined that the writ of habeas corpus in his case was ignored and therefore he was detained unconstitutionally. Bida was brought to trial, where a highly paid, bombastic lawyer portrayed Sister Dorothy as a subversive, who was working for the violent and imperialistic government of the United States. Playing to the pride of the Brazilian people, he shouted that Dorothy was being used to protect American corporate interests. In spite of the vigorous defense and the fact that the convicted gunmen reversed their testimony against Bida, he was convicted and sentenced to thirty years in prison.[25] This was the first time in over seven hundred cases in Para that a rancher was convicted and imprisoned for ordering a killing

Typical of the local justice system, Bida was acquitted and set free in 2008 at another trial, where Raifran changed his testimony and said he killed the nun for personal reasons.[26] Dot's brother, David, who has been to Brazil many times and has become her dedicated advocate, called the acquittal "appalling."

In December of 2008, Galvao, the wealthy rancher and alleged co-architect of Dorothy's murder was arrested and charged with her slaying. There is strong evidence against Galvao and he was to be tried in early 2009.[27]

In April 2009, a three-judge panel in the northern state of Para voted unanimously to arrest and retry Bida. The judges also voted to retry Raifran. Only time will tell whether the struggling and often corrupt justice system in that part of Brazil will be able to bring all the guilty parties in Dorothy's murder to justice.

An Enduring Legacy

Dorothy's legacy still lives on. She has been awarded a number of honorary degrees and has received tributes from the United Nations and the United States Congress, and she has received many awards. But most importantly, Dot's legacy lives on in Amazonia: in the union of the farmers, the women's association, the many schools she built. Sister Dorothy gave self-esteem and confidence to so many of her people, and taught them ways to sustain their magnificent surroundings. Even though local loggers and ranchers have been angered by all the international attention given to their area, and have stepped up their pressure to gain land, the common people have been inspired by Dorothy and empowered to carry on their resistance in the face of increased dangers and threats.

Many in the area say that they miss Dot's bright smile as she drove up to their huts on her motorcycle. They fondly remember the clear ring of her voice, as she joined hands with her beloved poor and led them in prayer. Those who knew her will never forget her strong voice, speaking up for their human dignity, and for their rights to the land. Like so many women before her, like Mother Teresa, Saint Julie, and Dorothy Day, Irma Dorothy Stang gave her all for the poorest of the poor. As a member of her community Sister Elizabeth, wrote: "Her life tells us that we too can free ourselves from the slavery of consumerism and live more simply so that others can simply live. Dorothy Stang, a little lady from Ohio, has a big message for the world."[28]

chapter four

Father Pedro Arrupe, s.j.

It was August 7, 1945, the day after the doomsday attack on Hiroshima, Japan, by the first atomic bomb. Hundreds of the victims had come or were brought to the Jesuit house for care. A young Jesuit, trained as a doctor, had been attending to their horrible wounds. When he offered his morning Mass, the chapel floor was crammed with men, women, and children, some with their flesh hanging from their bodies, and others with ghastly radiation wounds. As he turned toward the people with his arms outstretched, he was momentarily paralyzed by the sight of suffering and terrified at how science could be used to destroy life. After Mass, he continued caring for the many patients and made repeated trips into the city to help other victims of the bombing and bring more back to the Jesuit residence. Six months later all but two of the victims cared for by the Jesuits survived and were able to leave the makeshift hospital. Many of them asked to become Christians because they were inspired by the heroic and loving care they had received from the Jesuit community.

The young Jesuit was Father Pedro Arrupe, whose life was touched by an amazing span of world events: the Spanish Civil War, the rise of Nazism in Germany, Japan's entrance into World War II, and the dropping of the two atomic bombs. He would be elected superior general of the Jesuits and lead them through the challenging years of church renewal and world upheaval. Pedro was a man of destiny, a global figure who touched the lives of countless people, a priest dedicated to peace and justice.

Early Years

Pedro was born in 1907 in Bilbao, Spain, a large industrial city in the Basque country, which today houses a famous Guggenheim museum. Pedro was the youngest of five children. He lost his mother when he was only eight years old, and was raised by his father, an architect and journalist. The family was devoted to its Catholic faith. When Pedro was seventeen he began his medical studies in Madrid, and worked with the St. Vincent de Paul Society, feeding the poor in the slums of Madrid. The experience of filth, starvation, and squalor in these areas left an indelible mark on the young student and sharpened his sense of justice. When he was in medical school, Pedro was suddenly called home because his father was dying. The death was devastating for Pedro, for he had now lost both his parents. Life seemed to be collapsing around him.

Soon after his father's death, Pedro decided to accompany his sisters to Lourdes, where the shepherd girl Bernadette had experienced visions of Mary in 1858. Pedro hoped that the trip would take his mind off the loss of his father and offer him a break from his intense medical studies. He was struck by the great throngs at the shrine and by the numerous sick and disabled being brought on stretchers and in wheelchairs by attendants. Pedro had heard much about the miraculous cures at Lourdes and offered his medical services in some of the cases. During one of the processions, a nun whose spine was being eaten away by disease cried out: "I'm cured!" The crowds burst into a loud ovation. Pedro, as a physician, was able to examine the nun and her X-rays, and was deeply moved by the healing.[1] A few days later Pedro witnessed the cure of an elderly woman who had advanced stomach cancer and the healing of a paralyzed young man. Pedro had experienced the intense power of God first in the slums of Spain and now at the shrine of Lourdes.

When Pedro returned to his medical studies, he was a changed person. With both parents gone, he felt orphaned, adrift, and facing ultimate questions about what to do with his life. He felt that he was being called to heal spiritual ills, rather than physical ones. When Pedro announced that he was going to leave medical school and become a priest, his fellow students and professors thought he had lost his senses. Many of them were unbelievers and could not see how Pedro could give up a promising career to be a cleric in the church. The dean was so indignant that he refused to grant Pedro the "best student award," and the sum of money that went along with it. Unperturbed, Pedro withdrew from his medical studies, entered the Jesuit novitiate and donned a cassock. During his novitiate the same dean showed up and humbly explained that by withholding the award he had hoped to dissuade Pedro from giving up a brilliant medical career. The professor expressed his fondness for Pedro and the two men embraced in reconciliation.

During his training for the priesthood, Pedro felt a calling to follow the example of the Jesuit Francis Xavier and become a missionary to Japan. He wrote for permission to do this, but received a vague answer that it would be taken under consideration. Pedro stoically accepted the response and continued his studies, now amid serious social turmoil in Spain. Labor unions battled in the streets, the king stepped down, and a socialist regime hostile to the church took over. The Society of Jesus was dissolved in Spain, their assets confiscated, and their members forced to leave the country. Pedro had to move to spartan facilities in Belgium to continue his studies. By this time he had become a leader among his peers. When a flu epidemic broke out among them, he used his medical training to care for the afflicted.

Pedro was given permission during his last year of philosophy study to go to Holland to study medical ethics. While there he was selected to present several papers at an international congress in Vienna. He spoke before some of the foremost scholars in the world, astonished them with his youthful erudition, and received rave reviews for his presentations.

He returned to his studies and in 1936 was ordained to the priesthood. Soon after ordination Pedro was sent to the United States to study psychiatry. As he sailed from Europe, he left behind a Germany dominated by Adolf Hitler and the Nazis, an Italy controlled by Benito Mussolini's fascists, and a Spain locked in a bloody civil war and under the control of the dictator Francisco Franco. Pedro arrived in a United States that was struggling with economic depression. He studied psychiatry in Washington, D.C., and finished his Jesuit formation in Cleveland. During that period he received the hoped-for assignment to Japan.

Mission in Japan

In 1938 Pedro arrived in Japan. It was a lonely period for him, finding himself in a foreign land with little knowledge of the language, and working with German priests with whom he was not able to converse. Pedro was just starting to get used to his work as a missionary, when suddenly he was arrested and imprisoned as a suspected spy. He spent an entire month in a dark, freezing cell furnished with only a sleeping mat. At one point, he was interrogated for thirty-seven hours:

"Why have you come to Japan?"
"To work for you and offer myself for you..."
"What are your diplomatic relations with the embassy?"
"I do not even know the ambassador."
"Oh."
"Where is your money?—in your bank?"
"I receive little money every month, not as a salary but as a kind of gift; my provincial sends it to me so that I may be able to eat."
"Hmmm."
Then the third question: "Where is your wife?" [2]

On and on went the military tribunal, getting nowhere and baffled by this mysterious "spy."

Pedro's days in prison were frightening. He got very little sleep, meager food and there was the constant banging and clanging of the locks and doors. His future was uncertain; the punishment for espionage was execution by firing squad, hanging, or beheading. He had also heard barbarous stories of how priests had been tortured in earlier times of persecution in Japan. They had been burned at the stake, immersed in boiling sulphur water, and even hung by their feet until dead! Pedro found consolation in meditation and prayer and the period became a time of deep spiritual experience for him. Years later he would reflect how in solitary confinement he carried on a dialogue "with the guest of my soul." He wrote: "It was beautiful—the solitude with Christ, a mystical experience, nothing in my cell, only me and Christ."[3]

On Christmas Eve, Pedro was feeling especially sad in his cell, when he heard a murmur of voices coming toward him. At first he was frightened, thinking that the guards were coming for him, but then he realized that it was the wonderful sound of his parishioners softly singing carols for him outside his window. They had come to bring Bethlehem to his cell!

Eventually, Pedro was released. He had become close to many of the guards and they were sad to see him leave—some even visited him after his release. Before he left prison, Pedro thanked the commander of the jail, who was astonished at being thanked for putting Pedro in jail. Pedro explained: "Because it was one of the greatest sufferings in life. I came to Japan to work and suffer for you, and you were, with the best will and intention, the cause of this suffering. I consider you one of my best benefactors." The commander had never experienced a prisoner quite like this one and he answered: "Father Arrupe, go away and work for us; this wonderful doctrine of yours could save Japan." Pedro wrote that this "was one of the most precious moments of his life."[4]

Hiroshima

Pedro's next assignment in Japan was to be a fateful one; he was made novice master at Nagatsuka on the outskirts of Hiroshima. He settled into his temple-like home amid thatch-roofed houses, began to gain fluency in Japanese, and immersed himself in the culture. He learned the Zen tea ceremonies, became friends with the local Buddhist monks, and began to pray in the Eastern posture. (He used this posture for the rest of his life.) Pedro worked hard to teach his Jesuit candidates and also preached to make converts in the neighborhood. As the war dragged on, living became more difficult and food was scarce. Pedro found that he had to spend more time in the fields planting and harvesting food for his students. He also did some of the cooking and at times had to settle for serving the community only flour cakes and tea.

Armageddon

On the morning of August 6, 1945, Pedro was awakened as usual by the drone of an American B-29 on reconnaissance. The people of Hiroshima were used to having bombers fly over and the alarms going off, but they usually ignored the warnings. Bombers had been relentlessly attacking Tokyo and other Japanese cities for months, but always bypassed Hiroshima. It wasn't because that city was unimportant militarily. It was a main military center, the port where each week thousands of troops embarked, and it was encircled by heavy industry.

Pedro got up, sat cross-legged on his mat for morning prayer and then offered his usual Mass in the chapel. The air-raid sirens went off again at 6:00 AM and then again at 7:00 AM, but people just went about their business. In fact, many used to make fun of the planes, calling them "American airmail." They knew little of the bombings elsewhere and from the propaganda they received, they thought Japan was easily winning the war against the United States. Several more planes passed over, but the sirens were ignored as people bicycled to work and children ran barefoot to school with their lunch boxes and their compulsory cotton air raid helmets and first-aid kits. At 8:06 AM two B-29s appeared, flying very high over the city, one banking right, the other left. Three tiny parachutes blossomed from beneath one plane. Not knowing that these were measuring instruments for the bomb, and instead thinking that the pilots were bailing out in trouble, many below cheered. Suddenly, a huge bomb dropped from one of the planes, and then both planes peeled off and disappeared. The most horrendous weapon yet designed by man was about to be unleashed on the people of Hiroshima. Eighteen-hundred feet above the ground the bomb was detonated. In milliseconds an enormous lightning flash that became a huge ball of flame engulfed all below. Then a thunderous shockwave followed by a gigantic mushroom cloud, two miles in diameter, that rose up to the sky 60,000 feet high, its round summit seething and boiling with a white creamy foam.

The bomb had exploded directly over the Shima Hospital downtown. Those under the nuclear explosion were immediately vaporized and the shadows of those fleeing were etched on the sides of bridges and the few walls left standing like some sort of grotesque graffiti. Some victims were instantly liquefied, their skin melting off their frames, while others were so scorched that their clothes etched an eerie kind of tattoo on their bodies. Tens of thousands of buildings were leveled and as far as four miles away houses caught fire and collapsed. Of the city's population of 250,000, nearly half died instantly, including 20,000 children in schools in the heart of the city. Another 150,000 died within days from burns, open sores, and early radiation sickness.[5]

Pedro was preparing for class, when a blinding light filled his room. He had just been reading the gospel passages about the end times, and it seemed like something like that was going on now. As he opened the door to look toward the city, he heard an enormous explosion and a blast of hot air blew him across the room, where he lay covered with glass, plaster, and debris. The clock across the room was frozen at 8:10 AM. He staggered to his feet and ran to see how his students had survived. Fortunately, though some were bleeding from flying glass, none were seriously hurt. Pedro looked outside, now sure that a bomb had been dropped, but there was no sign outside of an explosion. The trees and flowers and rice paddies were still untouched. He then looked toward the city and saw clouds of smoke and high pillars of flames leaping toward the darkened sky. As he climbed to a higher position, Pedro could see that the city and many of its people had been obliterated.

Looking down the road, Pedro saw hundreds of people, bleeding, burned, blistered, and staggering toward the Jesuit house. The Jesuits converted their chapel and then the library into hospital rooms. As more arrived, the bedrooms, garden, and fields around the house were used for the suffering. Clothes, sheets, towels, and anything that could be found were torn up for bandages, and Pedro used his medical training and the house's limited medical supplies to attend to the patients. The seminarians raided their gardens and also scoured the area for food for the victims. All through this, the people murmured *pika-don,* which means "flash-bang," a description of the horrendous experience of the explosion.

Once matters were relatively under control, Pedro and several others ventured into the city to see how they could help. The sights and sounds were sickening. People were writhing in pain on top of others and crying for help; many were lying next to the river trying to bathe their wounds and drink from the filthy water, where body parts floated. Babies and small children cried for their mothers, and parents were staggering about in agony and grief searching for their children. Parents lay face down, clutching their burned babies. Many of the mangled dead were strewn across the land, as though slaughtered on a battlefield. Pedro did what he could to help the suffering and the dying, but it was nearly a hopeless cause. Eventually, he led those who could walk back to the Jesuit house, where they could rest and be treated.[6]

In the following days, Pedro administered to the many victims, often performing surgery, setting limbs, and removing shards of glass and pieces of wood from the patients. Days after, a new illness began to appear, caused by the radiation. People would get very cold, sores would appear in their mouths, and their hair would fall out. The very cells of their organs and bodies were breaking down. Soon many of them died. This radiation illness presented extraordinary challenges to Father Arrupe and his community.

Pedro soon learned that an atomic bomb had been dropped on his city, and then came to learn that another, equally devastating, had been dropped on another Japanese city, Nagasaki. Then, an enormous typhoon further devastated Hiroshima, destroying what was left of the city and claiming even more victims.

Post-war Mission
In September, Japanese surrender ceremonies took place and in the following month Americans began to occupy the area where Pedro lived. The Jesuits began their rebuilding during the painful time of Japanese recovery. Though the American troops behaved honorably, winning over many of the vanquished people, there were severe food shortages and many medical challenges. Pedro continued to work with his novices, whose ranks swelled with Japanese veterans returning from the war. He realized the war had created a spiritual vacuum, so he began translating spiritual classics from John of the Cross and Francis Xavier into Japanese.

Soon Pedro was transferred to Tokyo. On a visit to Rome in 1950 he was asked to travel to Europe and the United States, speaking on his experience of the atomic bomb and raising funds. In 1954 Pedro was elected vice-provincial of the Jesuits in Japan and later that year began his second journey around the world speaking on the bombing of Hiroshima. He continued these trips into the 1960s, all the while managing and expanding the Jesuit province in Japan. He watched as Japan rose from the ashes to become one of the most prosperous countries in the world.

Arrupe's experience of the atomic bomb in Hiroshima was transformative. As he relived it countless times in addresses around the world, he became more convinced of the horror and futility of war. He wrote:

> In the midst of so much destruction, confusion and corruption, the dark mystery of atomic radiation renders the screen of humanity clarescent, revealing both the fleshly futility of that which disappears like a shadow,

and the solidity, firmer than bone, of spiritual values.[7]

As he traveled around widely speaking on Hiroshima, he also became more keenly aware of global suffering and hunger. His mission from then on would be for peace and justice in the world.

The Second Vatican Council
In 1962 the Second Vatican Council opened and three years of intense discussion began on how to renew the church, set it to address the needs of the modern world, and work for peace and justice. The Council sought Jesuit reform: serving a populist church, returning to the original sources—Scripture and Ignatius' vision; an active concern for issues of the modern world; solidarity with the poor; collegiality; ecumenical and interfaith dialogue; and a vigorous commitment to freedom, peace, and justice. A number of Jesuits would play leading roles in the work of this Council: Karl Rahner in church reform; Henri de Lubac in the return to early sources; and John Courtney Murray in religious freedom. Always as a backdrop was the magnificent world vision of Pierre Teilhard de Chardin.

Little did Pedro suspect that he would be called upon to lead the Jesuits into this challenging and perilous era of reform as superior general. Already he had faced some of these issues during his tenure as leader in Japan. In fact, many of his German confreres objected to the open and liberal tendencies of his actions, and called for an investigation. For two years there was a close scrutiny of Arrupe's leadership and a report was sent to Rome in 1964. That same year the general of the Jesuits, Father Jean-Baptiste Janssens, died. Pedro was called to Rome, and elected superior general of the thirty-six thousand Jesuits around the world.

In his first interviews it was clear that Arrupe had a vision for the modern Jesuit. He approved of Teilhard de Chardin, whose work had been disparaged by the Vatican; he defended the young people of his time in their restlessness with the formality and legalism of their religion; and he stood with the progressive and activist Jesuits among his ranks. He said: "We fight...against the injustices and inequalities, especially in developing countries, as pointed out in the great encyclicals. Their workers give us food and then they die of starvation and malnutrition. We stand with them in their struggle for justice."[8] He was determined to lead the Jesuits in a passionate effort to confront the materialism, consumerism, and greed that were dehumanizing so many in the modern world. Liberation would be a key factor in his vision: "No longer are half measures and timid solutions admissible. He who today is not with Christ in the advancement and liberation of man, in the struggle against the sinful structures which torture man, is against Him."[9] Pedro firmly believed that silence toward this injustice was in fact a grave offense of complicity.

Early on in his tenure, Pedro traveled to visit Jesuits around the world, as well as many political and religious leaders. Most were charmed by his humility, humor, and grasp of world problems. They were impressed by his fluency in six languages, and his openness to new ideas and different religions was refreshing. When he spoke to large groups, he always touched on themes of social justice. At Fordham University in New York City, he spoke of human rights and freedom, as well as the need to speak a new language that is appropriate for the hearts of today's people. He met with civil rights leaders in the United States and assured them of his opposition to racism and challenged Jesuits to get more involved in interracial issues.

Pedro challenged the Jesuit educators in Latin America, pointing out that too often their schools were accessible only to the rich. He went to India and urged his confreres to train their people in modern methods of agriculture and industry. In Spain he founded an Institute for dialogue among believers and nonbelievers and urged them to listen and learn from each other. In 1968 he attended the historic meeting of Latin American bishops at Medellín, Columbia and joined his friend Dom Helder Camara in denouncing the flagrant injustices and violence that were widespread in Central and Latin America. He wrote to his men in these areas that, while he opposed their becoming militants or leaders of a party, they cannot ignore the economic or political dimensions of their work. He wrote:

Apoliticism, or systematic refusal of all presence in politics, is today impossible for the apostolic man. We cannot be silent, in certain countries, before regimes which constitute without any doubt a sort of institutionalized violence. We should denounce, with prudence but openly and clearly, policies inconsistent with "the global vision of humankind which the Church possesses in its own right."[10]

This perspective would later put him in opposition to the views of John Paul II and the Vatican.

During the years after the Council, the church, as well as the Jesuits, experienced a great deal of turmoil. Many Jesuits left the Society, often to marry, and the number of those entering plummeted. Arrupe remained calm and was stalwart in his belief in the Jesuit ideals. He urged his men to face the future, neither trying to go backward nor being swept aside by the winds of change that swirled around them. He encouraged them to constantly attend to their interior lives and be dedicated to prayer.

While in the United States in 1971 he pledged to the United Nations that Jesuits would be committed to working on global problems and would be dedicated to the common concerns of the human family. While there he also visited fellow Jesuit Daniel Berrigan, who had been imprisoned for burning draft records. Later he visited one of his men, an auxiliary bishop in Lima, Peru, who had been imprisoned for defending homeless demonstrators who had taken over a Jesuit school for shelter. In Brazil he joined his men in writing a document on liberation theology. In Ireland he gave a moving address on ecumenism, and in Russia he met with Russian Orthodox leaders. On a trip to Mexico Arrupe met with members of the Society to discuss their shift in educational goals

UNLIKELY SPIRITUAL HEROES

for teaching justice and educating for social change. In Africa he encouraged his men to engage in dialogue and collaboration with other religions. The Jesuits were now vigorously involved in the church of the modern world and their educational mission was to adapt to the "signs of the times." He wrote:

> Our students are not to see themselves as isolated individuals learning how to elbow their way through hostile masses to positions of power and prestige. Rather, let them discover in ways they can never forget that they are brothers and sisters in a planetary village, fellow pilgrims on spaceship earth.[11]

The Synod on Justice in the World, 1972

Pedro was encouraged when the Vatican held a Synod on Justice in 1971 and commented on its statements with enthusiasm. He pointed out that Catholics have to do more that just teach about justice, they have to actively witness to it. He believed that gospel love demands justice for the poor. Such action is needed for transformation of the world and, as the synod proclaimed, is "a constitutive dimension of the preaching of the gospel."[12] Christians must be involved in the struggle for human rights and on the side of the poor. This indeed is integral to Christian conversion, a radical change from the apathy and prejudice that keep us from serving the needy.[13] Pedro also asked the church to deal with its own members justly, pay fair wages, and offer just promotions to those who serve the church. He also called the hierarchy and clergy to a simple lifestyle, befitting followers of Jesus. Moreover, he appealed to all Christians to denounce oppression of minorities, prisoners, migrant workers, refugees, and the defenseless, and to oppose political systems that promote such oppression.

Men for Others

In 1973 Arrupe gave a significant address to former students of Jesuit schools and urged them to be "Men [and Women] for Others"—a motto that is still a powerful incentive in Jesuit institutes of learning today.

60

Here he picked up the theme that was given impetus by Vatican II and then grew intensively in the writings of Pope Paul VI and the radical statements of Latin American, Asian, and African bishops and in the synod. This was a clarion call for all Christians to radically change their lives and their actions and to work on behalf of social reform. Pedro calls for "liberation" to be central in the Christian way of life. Indeed Jesuit education is to develop students who resist accumulation and selfish interest, students who give of themselves to others. Pedro proclaims: "Only he who loves fully realizes himself as a man."[14] Loving and giving is the only way to become fully human.

The Jesuit General Congregation of 1976

Pedro led the Society of Jesus to officially commit Jesuits to working for social justice in their worldwide congregation in 1976. Justice was now to be an integral part of the Jesuit mission. This called for serious discernment about the original Ignatian ideals of "finding God in all things" and being "contemplatives in action." In order to be part of Vatican II renewal, the Jesuits needed to carefully read the "signs of the times" and through a process of discernment insert themselves into the modern world as authentic apostles, in solidarity with the poor.

Tragically, such commitments to justice and the poor would lead to the expulsion, persecution, and even execution of a number of Jesuits. The most notable was the cold-blooded killing of the six Jesuits, along with their housekeeper and her daughter, at the University of Central America in El Salvador in 1989. The Jesuits had followed Arrupe's leadership. They had lived simply in spare rooms at the university, and in class had raised the consciousness of their students about the oppression in El Salvador. On weekends some of them worked in solidarity with the peasants, listening to their stories of oppression. Then they would make public through the media what they had heard from their people about the injustices and atrocities perpetrated by their government. For this witness to justice, they paid with their lives.

For many Jesuits, this mission for justice would involve developing a new identity, one adapted to but not overwhelmed by today's culture; an identity that is deeply reflective, collaborative, and open to diversity and change. The Jesuits were being called from a lifestyle that had often been characterized as isolated, reserved, and superior to a new posture that was personal, friendly, and communal. They were called to move from a fidelity to rules to responsible freedom and personal initiative. Their educational methods should shift from "package" learning to a pedagogy of dialogue.[15] The new vision would be difficult for many of the members of the Society. Some would leave, others would dig in and refuse to adapt. But Pedro insisted on leading his men into the modern era as disciples of Jesus and Ignatius.

The End

In the summer of 1981, Pedro suffered a severe stroke and was incapacitated until his death ten years later. The great speaker fluent in six languages was now all but silenced; the outstanding leader was now seriously disabled. It was a difficult period for Pedro. He often experienced severe depression and was deeply saddened when the Vatican appointed his successor, rather than allowing the Jesuits to hold their usual election. This seemed a repudiation of his leadership, but Pedro accepted the decision with his usual grace and obedience. During his years of incapacitation he remained close to his Jesuit brothers. He often received visits from friends and from notables like Mother Teresa and John Paul II. He continued to inspire with his courage, charm, and compassion until February 5, 1991. That was the day that Pedro Arrupe passed on.

Father Arrupe left behind an army of religious men, as well as their countless students, whom he led into the church's social mission for peace and justice. Through the many Jesuit missions, schools, and universities throughout the world, his Ignatian followers are in the vanguard of those dedicated to the issues of peace, justice, equality of women, and care for the earth.

chapter five

Thomas Merton

It was an enigmatic death for one of the great spiritual writers of our time: He was found dead—electrocuted by a fan that lay across his naked body— in his hotel room in Bangkok, far from his Kentucky monastery. He had just showered after delivering a controversial lecture on "Marxism and Monastic Life." To add further irony, an SAC bomber, returning from the war in Vietnam, a war he had so vehemently protested, brought his body back to the States. Merton was buried by his many friends near the Gethsemani monastery chapel, next to the abbot with whom he had so often been at odds.

Thomas Merton, who as a young man had left the world to find his true self and then as an older monk returned to that world to remind it of its brutal human cruelty and violence, was gone.

Early Formation

Merton had an interesting pedigree. He was born during a snowstorm in Prades, France, on January 31, 1915, in the first winter of World War I. His father, Owen, was from New Zealand; his mother, Ruth, was an American. Both were artists who had met in Paris. Tom's mother was a Quaker of sorts, dedicated to pacifism, and no doubt touched him with her peaceful love and care. She strongly opposed Owen's involvement with the war. The threat of Owen being drafted triggered a decision to sail for the United States, and the family moved in with Ruth's parents.

In 1918 as the war was ending, their second son, John Paul, was born. He seemed to have stolen the spotlight from Tom, who remembered his mother turning cold to him at that time. His mother died of cancer when he was only six.

Tom was bounced around from place to place, often staying with relatives while his father pursued his art. He attended various English and French boarding schools. Early on he was known as something of a rebel.[1] Just before Tom's sixteenth birthday, his father died, leaving the teen alone in the world. On a solitary tour of Rome, Tom was drawn to the churches and had an experience of his father's presence, which moved him to prayer. Soon he turned to the Bible, and began to have some inkling that he might want to be a monk. Meanwhile, he read broadly and tested new ideas.

At eighteen, Tom entered Cambridge University, and while there he showed little interest in religion, but did continue to pray. He signed the Oxford Peace Pledge, declaring that he would not fight in any war. Tom's year at Cambridge included much drinking, partying, and carousing. Eventually, he fathered a child and later almost lost his scholarship. Before that could happen though, his disgraced and embarrassed godfather who had sponsored him at Oxford persuaded Tom to withdraw. Tom, himself, was disgraced and felt alienated from his godfather. As often before, Tom felt rejected.

Tom next enrolled in Columbia University in New York City, where he flourished as a student and writer, and made some lifelong friends. It was a fresh start and key time for finding out who he truly was. "Merty" grew into a charming and interesting person, who could both pound out jazz on the piano and enliven any party and be a serious student of languages and literature in the classroom. Tom also developed into a fine writer for the university magazines, and was ultimately elected editor of the yearbook and voted "Best Writer" by fellow students. He dabbled with communist literature and, though he felt it to be largely wrongheaded, communism seemed like the only political ideology concerned about workers and social justice. He picketed against Mussolini's invasion of Ethiopia and took part in a peace strike at the university.[2] The Spanish Civil War was dividing the student body, and Merton thought that, like all wars, it was a useless waste of life. Meanwhile, his grandparents who helped raise him in America passed away, leaving Tom more alone than ever.

At Columbia, Tom began reading Augustine's *Confessions* and Thomas a Kempis's *The Imitation of Christ* on the advice of, of all people, a Hindu monk. His graduate thesis on William Blake took him into religious experience and mysticism. Eventually, Tom moved toward an interest in Catholicism, and often slipped into the back of churches during Mass. Soon after he asked for instructions to enter the Catholic church, and he was baptized in November, 1938. Tom then took an exciting course on Thomism, the philosophical study of the works of Saint Thomas Aquinas, and met Jacques Maritain, a renowned Thomist at a lecture. During this time, Hitler was marching through Europe; Tom, however, immersed in religious studies, distanced himself from politics, and found himself discussing with friends his desire to be a priest.

Throughout his studies and religious conversion, Thomas continued to nurture his ambition to be a successful writer. He spent summers reading, writing, and partying with friends at a cottage near St. Bonaventure, in the Allegheny Mountains of New York. Back in New York City, he continued his studies, perfected his jazz piano skills, and became an expert dancer in the bars of Greenwich Village. Recovering from a party one morning, he was suddenly overwhelmed with a feeling of disgust with his lifestyle and decided to become a priest.[3] He was leery of the Jesuits, frightened by the Trappists, and felt drawn to the Franciscans. During the summer of 1938, he moved onto the campus of St. Bonaventure to consider the Franciscans, but after discussing his past with them, they turned him down. (Years later they may have regretted that decision!)

The war in Europe was heating up and, even though the United States had not yet entered the conflict, Tom was resolved that if he got drafted he would insist on being a noncombatant. He finished his master's at Columbia and began to seek employment. He heard of an opening at St. Bonaventure in English, and after interviewing with the saintly biblical scholar Father Thomas Plassman, O.F.M., he was offered a teaching position in 1939.

Tom got a fresh start with a full load of teaching that fall, and tried to join the friars in their religious services. His debut at teaching did not impress; he did not seem to connect with his students. Meanwhile, he continued to have romantic relationships.

The bombing of his beloved England distressed Tom and he grieved for the people, perhaps some of whom he might have known, who were killed. He had thoughts maybe he should be with them, fighting. He received his draft card from the government. Tom wrote to the Selective Service, asking for noncombatant status, as he put it: "[S]o as not to have to kill men made in the image of God…."[4] Soon after he was called in for his physical examination and was informed that he was not needed for the moment because of his exceptionally bad teeth.

Merton decided to make a retreat at the Trappist monastery at Gethsemani, Kentucky. He was instantly enthralled by its beauty and breathlessly wrote in his journal that this was the center of America, which held the country and the universe together.[5] While at the monastery, he read the life of Thérèse of Lisieux and was drawn to her simplicity and surrender to God. As inspiring as the retreat was, he was still filled with confusion and doubt. Tom returned home with difficult questions about war, racial injustice, and his own calling.

Catherine de Hueck Doherty
In the summer of 1941 Catherine de Hueck came to campus and berated those who attended her talk for being lazy and concerning themselves with studying dead subjects while the world was bleeding around them. She challenged them to live in poverty and minister to the

poor. The next day Merton asked Catherine if he could come to New York and help out at her Friendship House, serving the poor. She agreed and in August he showed up in Harlem. He worked there, sorting clothes and mopping floors, while he wrote about the wasted lives and alienation he saw around him. Tom concluded that white, middle-class Catholics who accepted racial prejudice were hypocrites. Tom listened intently to Catherine's impassioned pleas for lay service to the poor, and her challenges to religious who visited there about their apathy. She was a pioneer in lay ministry who introduced Tom to Catholic Action and sharpened his awareness of the plight of the poor. Tom then moved on from there to another retreat at Gethsemani. Now the need for social work that he had seen in Harlem made him think that being a monk would be an easy way out of all this. Catherine invited him to work with her and he toyed with the idea.

Back at St. Bonaventure, he began a correspondence with Catherine in which he at times rambles about his considering the lay vocation and sees Bonaventure like a golf course when juxtaposed with Harlem. Catherine continued to encourage him to work with her. In his letters to her, Tom questions whether social service doesn't have to be joined with political action; love with justice. In November, 1941, he wrote that teaching seemed to be a "sort of harmless hobby," and felt a higher calling. In early December, he commented that he wanted to be a Trappist, but had an "impediment" from his past that was driving him silly. He wrote: "I simply long with my whole existence to be completely consecrated to God in every gesture, every breath and every movement of my body and mind…." And this for him would be as a Trappist, but he feared that the draft would kill him first.[6]

At St. Bonaventure, Tom was relieved when told that in fact there was no impediment to his entering religious life. The draft board was hot on his tracks, so he had decided to go to Gethsemani and test his luck with the Trappists. On December 13 he wrote Catherine that he was a postulant at Gethsemani: "… it will no doubt be hard, but at least I will know there is nothing keeping me from God anymore—I can belong entirely to Him by simply consenting to each trial as it presents itself,…"[7] And trials there would be!

Gethsemani

Thomas Merton had left the world. He had entered a monastery of strict observance where there were endless hours of prayer, hard physical work, complete silence (the monks used sign language), meager diet, and regular fasting, exposure to extreme heat and cold, and exclusion of newspapers, radio, and films. He went in fully expecting to live the rest of his life in the enclosure and be buried there. Tom assumed the religious name Brother Louis.

Merton was allowed to write two hours a day in the scriptorium, usually on pious topics. In 1942 he published some poems and in 1944 he published his first book, *Thirty Poems*. Often he was assigned to write lives of the saints, guides about the monastery, histories of the order (*The Waters of Siloe*); he also kept a personal journal. In 1946 he began the autobiography that would thrust him into celebrity, *The Seven Storey Mountain*. He worked feverishly on this book and many other projects, passing sheets to a censor as he wrote them. In 1948 he published six books, but the only memorable one was *The Seven Storey Mountain*. Off to a slow start, the book gradually built up momentum and then became a best-seller. Merton was famous and letters flooded into the monastery where he had gone to live in seclusion. The "world" was coming back!

Merton's writing was now much in demand and he continued to offer more books, usually on religious life and contemplation. He was ordained in 1949 and two years later was appointed master of scholastics, who was responsible for training and advising the professed monks. During his five years in that position he published three books on religious life and a number of articles and poems.

In 1955 Merton was appointed master of novices, a serious position that he held for ten years. During that period and into the early sixties, he continued to produce an avalanche of books, articles, and poems, mostly on spiritual matters. After that, Merton turned his attention to social issues.

Attention to Worldly Matters

Merton's consciousness of social issues emerged gradually. It arose in the midst of a tension he felt between defending the isolation of the monastery and embracing an active concern for the oppressed. In 1956 he had begun taking notes on Gandhi and nonviolence. The poems and ideas of one of his confreres, Ernesto Cardenal, helped him understand the plight of the poor and oppressed in Central America. He was also horrified by details of the Nazi death camps and the atomic bombing of Japan.[8] Merton's earlier concern for social issues before he joined the Trappists was reignited. He began to have a new appreciation for himself and now wanted to extend himself to others. In 1958 he wrote: "My Catholicism is all the world and all ages."[9] That same year he wrote a passage in this journal that would become classic when he used it ten years later in his *Conjectures of a Guilty Bystander:*

> Yesterday in Louisville, at the corner of 4th and Walnut, suddenly realized that I loved all the people and that none of them were, or could be totally alien to me. As if waking from a dream—the dream of my separateness, of my "special" vocation to be different. My vocation does not really make me different from the rest of men or just one in a special category....[10]

In his journal Merton was returning to solidarity with the human community. At the same time, he was wrestling with his perennial problem of wanting to live as a hermit. By the time he wrote *Conjectures*, published in 1965, Merton was fully involved in the issues of peace and justice.

By 1960 Merton was resigned to the fact that his strenuous efforts to join an order of hermit-monks were fruitless and he was given permission to spend a few hours each day in a hermitage in the woods near the monastery. Although the demands on him for writing of all kinds were extreme, he began to publish articles on racial prejudice and nuclear war. Merton had decided that the modern mystic and prophet should not be outside of and remote from the world. True mysticism should not be a rejection of the human race so that one can seek salvation. Authentic worship was not praying for the world without an awareness of its problems. Merton observed that contemplatives need not leave the cloister and can come to "understand the world's anguish and share in it in their own way…."[11]

This involvement in "worldly" matters was not an easy decision for Merton. He would get resistance from his superiors, who did not particularly want him to be a voice in controversial worldly matters. It would change his image from being the holy contemplative monk to being that of the radical protester. He would alienate people, especially Cold War patriots who expected him to defend the United States against the Soviet Union, but instead were hearing him condemn both countries for endangering the world with nuclear arms.

Merton was devastated by the very thought of Auschwitz and wrote scathing condemnations of it. One of his most powerful was "Auschwitz: A Family Camp," exposing the utter duplicity about what went on in the camp on the part of those put on trial for the atrocities there.[12] He also wrote a biting piece on how the "exterminating equipment" used in the camp was ordered in such a civil, business-like fashion.[13]

The Cold War

In the early sixties the United States was locked into a Cold War with the Soviet Union, which included a nuclear arms race. Merton was alarmed at the brink of destruction that faced the world and wrote about it extensively. He could be apocalyptic in his depiction of the situation. He feared that the whole world was "plunging headlong into frightful destruction." He declared that "this is true war-madness, an illness of the mind and spirit that is spreading with a furious and subtle contagion all over the world."[14] For Merton, America was the most seriously afflicted, with its bomb shelters and paranoia. He thought we had entered a "post-Christian era," where we had lost our values of love and peace. For him the only choice was to abolish war through prayer and sacrifice, through a willingness to restrain our instinct for violence. He proclaimed: "It is the great Christian task of our time."[15]

Merton mocked America's self-righteous "prayers for peace" as it headed toward murderous destruction. He had challenging words for his fellow citizens: "…[I]nstead of hating the people you think are warmongers, hate the appetites and the disorder in your own souls, which are the causes of war. If you love peace, then hate injustice, hate tyranny, hate greed—but hate these things in *yourself,* not in another."[16] He called upon America to heed its peace tradition of the Quakers, Thoreau, and Martin Luther King, Jr.[17] He strongly supported the civil rights movement as a significant drive for peace in the United States and was one of the first to raise early alarms about the potentially violent racial issues in America.[18] He was also sympathetic to the struggles of Native Americans and called for justice in recognizing their rights.[19]

Merton's "War and the Prayer for Peace" is another example of how he did not spare criticism of his own country when it came to warmongering.

> When I pray for peace I pray to God to pacify not only Russians and the Chinese but above all my own nation and myself.… I am not just praying that the Russians will give up without a struggle and let us have our own way. I am praying that both we and the Russians may somehow be restored to sanity and learn how to work out our problems, as best we can, together, instead of preparing for global suicide.[20]

In 1962 Merton published an article "Target Equals City" in mimeographed form that caused his superiors much consternation and brought a directive to him to stop writing on war and peace. He pointed out that World War II had been considered a "just war" that faced the unjust aggression of Germany, Italy, and Japan. Then the distinction between civilian and combatant was dropped, as the Allies began obliteration bombing and then dropped two atomic bombs.

Merton rejects the justification for this tactic, which was done to break the enemy's morale and will to resist. He described such bombing as "pure terrorism."

Merton was also outraged that such immoral behavior was appearing in attitudes toward nuclear war. He believed that the United States had in fact adopted the same methods as the enemies it felt so justified in stopping. He could be extreme in his attacks on America, calling it a "sick nation," whose power "has gone beyond all the bounds of natural law and human rights."[21] Moreover, he was shocked that so many American Catholics were involved in justifying nuclear war against the U.S.S.R. in order to save America from communism. He urged Catholics in America to turn from such belligerence and the glorification of war to become nonviolent resisters and confronters in the cause of peace.[22]

Merton saw this headlong rush toward war as unchristian. He concluded: "There is only one winner in war. That winner is not justice, not liberty, not Christian truth. The winner is war itself."[23] This was radical stuff. Merton was not only challenging the American position on nuclear war, he was contesting the legitimacy of the Allies' tactics in winning the Second World War. Many Americans objected, most American bishops were displeased, and Merton's superiors came down on him and he was forbidden to write on war and peace in April 1962. (Some of his materials continued to come out in mimeograph form and at times Merton wrote under pseudonyms.)

Just before he was silenced, Merton wrote another controversial article, which he had revised a number of times fully knowing how divisive it would be. In this piece, he pointed out how the times were indeed apocalyptic, in that the United States and U.S.S.R. were prepared on a moment's notice to annihilate each other and the world. He appealed to the teaching of John XXIII that Christians must use every means at their disposal to strive for peace at this dangerous time. He lamented the fact that "we are no longer living in a Christian world." Instead, Christians on both sides of the Iron Curtain had the same moral sickness, rooted in a materialistic view of life. They had become opportunistic and pragmatic, morally blind, and irresponsible. Merton depicted his contemporaries as stumbling along, sometimes with the best intentions. None of the former rules apply. In nuclear war there are only losers, so desperately he called for the restoration of moral sense and for major efforts toward disarmament. Merton maintained that the church could no longer see nuclear war as limited, for it is uncontrolled annihilation and stands condemned by its own nature. For Merton, nuclear war was mass genocide. He called on Christians to stop being ambiguous and compromising and to protest clearly and forcibly against such atrocities.[24]

During the same period, Merton wrote in *The Catholic Worker* how distressed he was that Catholics had come to justify a nuclear first strike against the U.S.S.R. in order to preserve their religious freedom. It was as though they saw themselves in a holy war, when in fact they were heading toward global destruction. He couldn't understand why his position and that of others opposed to nuclear arms was considered so disloyal and radical when in fact papal teaching going back to Pius XII deplored every form of unlimited and "indiscriminate destruction in war, whether by nuclear or by conventional weapons."[25] By his own admission, Merton was strident on the issue of nuclear war and sometimes tended to "lash out with a baseball bat."[26]

Merton's passion in his war writing can make us realize just how passive many of us have become with regard to nuclear weapons. During Merton's years, many Catholics had become accustomed to the legitimacy of a "first strike" against the Soviet Union in order to preserve our way of life. Merton thought that to be insane, due to the massive destructive power of nuclear weapons. In contrast, many today are simply in denial about the dangers of nuclear warfare. The United States and Russia still have tens of thousands of nuclear warheads pointed we-are-not-sure where. But now in addition, Israel, England, France, India, Pakistan, and China have nuclear weapons. North Korea and Iran are on their way. Small nuclear weapons can be assembled by terrorists. In a sense, there is more danger than in Merton's day, yet less share in his passionate concern than did during his lifetime.

In many ways, Merton was prophetic in his attitudes toward nuclear war. His perspectives on war and peace were given confirmation when John XXIII agreed with much of what he said in his papal encyclical *Pacem in Terris* in 1963. (Merton wrote his abbot general and said that it was a good thing the pope did not have to go through the Trappist censors and asked to resume writing about peace issues again.) His silencing began to thaw after that.[27]

Nonviolence
Merton embraced nonviolence when he was a young man and then wrestled with it throughout his life. Merton regretted that pacifists were so often portrayed as cowards, pathetic idiots, or oddballs. Instead, he thought that genuine pacifists fulfilled the ideals of the Sermon on the Mount and authentic Christian tradition. This tradition obligates Christians to follow the law of love and therefore to make use of nonviolent means whenever possible. Merton points out that pacificism is not passive acquiescence, and that there are times when nonviolent resistance is impossible and force "may and should be used."[28] He wrote Dorothy Day, an absolute pacifist, that her position was of immense importance, but he had some reservations: "It is true that I am not theoretically a pacifist. That only means that I do not hold that a Christian *may not* fight, and that a war *cannot* be just. I hold that there is such a thing as a just war."[29] At the same time, he believed the Cold War and the other wars going on then were filled with evil, falsity, and injustice. Merton believed that love and mercy are the most powerful forces on earth and that Christians are obliged to have these forces dominate their lives. Like Jesus, his disciples should be willing to sacrifice themselves for others.

Merton was devoted to Gandhi's teaching on nonviolence.[30] He held that lying is the mother of violence. A truthful person simply cannot remain violent, nor can that person really discover the truth while being violent. Merton taught that if we believe the propaganda about our enemy, we will feel justified in being violent. Moreover, if we are false to the authentic goodness and love within us, we will be inclined toward violence. Falsity and violence are not natural to humans and are not a source of happiness. Consistent with Merton's constant search for his true self, he was convinced that if he were true to himself and to the innate goodness of others, he would not be violent.[31]

Merton found it ironic that Christianity was able to overcome the Roman Empire with nonviolence, but, once it was embraced Christianity became violent. He says: "The heroism of the soldier supplanted the heroism of the martyr." The supreme sacrifice was then to die fighting for the emperor and the cross became united with the sword, to the extent that even popes and monks went into battle. The Crusades and the conquistadores slaughtered under the sign of the cross. Christian militancy had become the norm and the nonviolence of the gospel was forgotten or even rejected.[32]

Nonviolence for Merton was not some novel tactic that edifies without being marred by blood and avoids confronting ugly and evil behavior. It is a readiness to suffer evil and face even death for the defense of truth and human beings.[33] It is based on the essential unity of humans and dedicated to healing and reconciliation. It is indeed a power that transforms human beings and society.

At the same time, Merton was critical of pacifists who used their philosophy as a weapon against others, and believed they had not dealt with the struggle of violence within themselves.[34] For a time he removed himself as a sponsor of the Catholic Peace Fellowship when a young pacifist immolated himself in front of the United States mission to the United Nations.[35] He even became reluctant to describe himself as a pacifist because of the extreme views that had attached themselves to that label.

Merton set down seven conditions for the practice of nonviolence:

1. That it be based on transformation of the present state and therefore not linked to unjust use of power.

2. That those from powerful nations be nonviolent not for themselves, but for others who are poor and underprivileged.

3. In the case of nuclear war there should be no self-righteousness on the part of the wealthy nations which can harden into war-making.

4. That nonviolence be presented as a possible and desirable alternative to violence, and that there be an openness to reasonable discussion with adversaries.

5. That truth be the goal and therefore, dishonest, violent, inhumane, or unreasonable means are avoided.

6. That we be open-minded and willing to learn from our adversaries.

7. That there be a radical hope in the sound possibilities in everyone and that love and grace can have the power to bring out these possibilities. For the Christian this is a hope in humanity and in the power of God.[36]

There was no question about it for Merton: Peacemaking was at the heart of the Christian mission. It was the mission that Jesus gave his followers: "The Christian is and must be by his very adoption as a son of God, a peacemaker (Matt. 5:9). He is bound to imitate the Savior who, instead of defending himself with twelve legions of angels (Matt. 26:55), allowed himself to be nailed to the Cross and died praying for his executioners."[37]

Eventually, Merton's prophetic call for peace was joined with the teachings of John XXIII, Paul VI, and Vatican II and the Catholic peace movement became a strong force in this country.[38] The well-known pacifist Gordon Zahn maintains that many of Merton's prophetic positions on peace were echoed in the American bishops' historic pastoral *The Challenge of Peace*.[39]

Vietnam

Merton was sickened by the Vietnam Conflict and became an ardent protester. He wrote letters where he described the conflict as poisonous, unjust, and based on brutal untruth. In another letter he declared that America has to learn that destructive power cannot build a world of peace and urged reason, negotiation, and peaceful settlement.[40] In a letter to President Lyndon B. Johnson, he stated:

> As a priest and monk of the Catholic Church I would like to add my voice to the voices of all those who have pleaded for a peaceful settlement in Vietnam. A neutralized and united Vietnam protected by secure guarantees would certainly do more for the interests of freedom and of the people of Southeast Asia, as well as for our own interests, than a useless and stupid war.[41]

In an article in *The Catholic Worker* in March, 1968, Merton relates how several members of the International Volunteer Service in Vietnam had resigned and returned to America, protesting that the United States was needlessly ravaging Vietnam. They had seen the horrible damage of napalm spraying, which was "death by roasting or suffocation." Americans, he wrote, are fed propaganda on how we are saving these people from communism, when in fact we are burning and bulldozing their homes, fields, and crops and driving many into unlivable situations. He was convinced that America, instead of fighting communism, was in fact strengthening it and driving the Vietnamese toward Red China. Instead of being at war, as some would have it, out of love, it was being waged out of American "inner violence" and "psychopathic delusions." It was a war with "overwhelming atrocities."[42]

In December of that same year, Merton decided to find some inner peace from all the turmoil and violence in his world. He set out on a long hoped-for journey to further explore Eastern religions. Once again, he was trying to understand Eastern methods of contemplation and to compare them to his own. As the Dalai Lama once said in a lecture in

Berea College in Kentucky, Merton was intent on building bridges between Western and Eastern spiritualities.

Suddenly and tragically, Merton's passionate and winding search for peace and truth came to an end on that trip. Merton was accidentally electrocuted in his living quarters in Bangkok. The mystic and profound advocate for contemplative life, sensitive poet, devoted friend to many, tireless correspondent, prophetic promoter of peace and justice was silenced. Yet, Merton still lives on in the legacy of his writing, which he always held was his deepest calling.

chapter six

Father Maximilian Kolbe, O.F.M.

When the prisoners of Auschwitz's Block 14 heard there was an escape, their faces went white. First those in the escapee's block were required to stand at attention in the parade grounds until the escapee was found. If the person was not found by curfew, the prisoners were sent to the barracks without food. The next day the "stand-out" was carried out again in the hot sun without food. Many were overcome with heat and hunger and were dragged to the side and piled together. In the afternoon there was a short break, some food was given, and it was announced that the escapee had not been found. The prisoners knew the next step. Ten prisoners, sometimes more, would be selected to die of starvation and thirst in the "Death Block."

The hated Commander Karl Fritzsch liked this part of the drill. Slowly he walked along the lines, knowing that he had the power of life or death, and would point to one terrified person and then another until he had ten. At one point, one of the "chosen" broke down and cried out that he would never see his wife and children again. There was a long silence, and then against all rules of the yard, a man stepped toward Fritzsch and said something in a low voice.

One nearby witness has given this account of the event: The Commander said: "What does this Polish swine want?" A frail but determined prisoner named Maximilian Kolbe pointed to the prisoner that had been selected and said: "I am a Polish Catholic priest. I am old. I want to take his place, because he has a wife and children." Kolbe wisely knew that the Nazis hated priests, and had no use for the feeble elderly. Even though Kolbe was only forty-seven, he knew that "the old priest" combination would appeal to the commanders. Our witness says that Fritzsch was speechless and surprised at the audacity of this priest. When the officer got back his composure, he ordered Kolbe to step out and be part of the ten. The family man's life was saved and the ten victims were marched off to the Death Block.[1]

Maximilian Kolbe is best remembered for this incident where he took another man's place in the death chamber at Auschwitz. This alone qualifies him as a hero, but there is much more to Kolbe's life that is also inspiring. He started a major reform movement among his fellow Franciscans, ran an enormous religious publishing business that spread the gospel throughout Poland, and provided shelter and protection for many refugees and Jews during the Nazi occupation of Poland in World War II.

To understand Kolbe as a hero of our time one must dig beneath his traditional Polish piety, a piety which in its fervor even put off many of his own Franciscans. His total dedication to Mary, "the Immaculata," and his organization of a militia of knights to conquer the world for her must be translated into Kolbe's strong discipleship with Jesus and his mother, as well as his passionate commitment to the gospel mission to teach all nations.

Early Life
Raymond Kolbe (Maximilian was his Franciscan name) was born in 1894 in a small village in Poland. His parents, Julius and Marianna, were weavers, and worked long hours at the loom in their home. Like so many skilled weavers in developing countries today, they produced magnificent pieces, only to see most of the profits go to the wholesalers. Raymond learned to be proud of his Polish background and hopeful that his country would be one day liberated from its occupation by

Russia, Austria, and Germany. Raymond's father was involved in the Polish underground and taught Raymond and his two brothers to play soldier and to be prepared to throw off the yoke of the Russians who occupied their part of Poland.

Typically, the family was also devoted to Jesus' mother, Mary, and they had a shrine to her in the house. The family devotion also extended to Saint Francis and his mission to serve the poor. When Raymond was only thirteen he decided to join the Franciscans, even if it meant sneaking out of the Russian zone to the Austrian zone where the friars were allowed to flourish. He began his studies in the bustling city of Lwon and excelled in math and science. In his spare time he helped design fortifications against the Russians, hoping to take part in the liberation of his country. Upon graduation, Raymond had decided to leave the friars and become a Polish soldier, but a visit from his mother persuaded him to remain a Franciscan. He began his novitiate training and took the name Maximilian.

Rome

Since he was such a promising student, Maximilian was sent to continue his seminary studies in Rome at the famous Gregorian University amid the splendor of the Vatican.

While Maximilian was occupied with his studies, World War I broke out. His father, Julius, and his brother joined the war effort, and his father was captured (and probably executed) by the Russians. While millions died in the trenches of Europe, Maximilian's student life in Rome was relatively undisturbed, except for the street skirmishes between papal supporters and those who backed government control of Rome. He also had to contend with the anticlericalism and organized demonstrations of the Freemasons.

Tuberculosis

In 1917 Maximilian contracted tuberculosis; he would be plagued with it throughout his life, to the point where he lost one lung. The initial signs came when Maximilian was playing football and began coughing up blood. After only a few months of recuperation, he was sent back to his studies. (There was little tolerance of illness in the religious life of those days.)

A New Crusade

During his recuperation period, Maximilian hatched an idea which he hoped would both reform his order and begin a movement that, with the idealism of a young seminarian, would change the world. It would be called the "Militia of the Immaculate," composed of "knights" dedicated to the conversion of sinners and the sanctification of all people. Rather than going to war for the freedom of his country, young Kolbe preferred to fight with the "weapons" of love and service. During this period, Maximilian was ordained and earned his second doctorate, this time in theology. He then returned to Poland in 1919.

Return to War-torn Poland

Maximilian returned to a country that was now once again independent, but which had been devastated by the war. Millions had died, and the economy was in ruins. Kolbe was assigned to teach in the Franciscan seminary in Kraków and used this opportunity to enlist many young men into his new organization. Immediately he received resistance from some of the older friars, who saw Maximilian as a sickly and naïve rookie who was idealistically trying to save the world with his fledgling pious organization.[2] In his letters, Maximilian expresses the pain that such criticism and betrayal gave him. He noted that his work at times became tiresome and even frightening, and that only his faith in God and his devotion to Mary offered him the support and foundation to go on.[3] The organization continued to draw members from convents, colleges, and even the military academy. The numbers grew into the hundreds and then the thousands. The organization, on a smaller scale, paralleled the success of the Legion of Mary which started in Ireland, spread throughout the world, and became strong in the United States.

A Relapse

In 1920 Maximilian had a tubercular relapse, and was no longer able to teach. He was sent to sanatoriums for fourteen months. Yet, even in the convalescent homes, Maximilian kept in touch with his militia through correspondence and was active in preaching the gospel and ministering to the patients who surrounded him. As he grew stronger, he even began to visit another sanatorium for university students, ministering to them even though it was not welcomed by the atheistic administration. When they attempted to stop him, Maximilian firmly reminded them that "I was a guest like anyone else and I had the right to come during visiting hours."[4] One time he even felt well enough to extend his friendship and compassion to a group of Russian prisoners of war encamped near his hospital.

At one point, an erroneous report of Maximilian's death reached Rome. A requiem Mass was said for him and the rector of his college wrote a striking and prescient obituary saying: "He was an angel, a young saint, full of fervor and zeal, one of the most pious, edifying and scholastically gifted students that this college has ever had."[5] It turned out that the rumor of Maximilian's death was highly exaggerated, and Maximilian was able to return to Kraków and resume his teaching position and the leadership of his militia.

Starting a Magazine

Maximilian was able to get permission from his superiors to start a militia magazine on the proviso that he finance it himself. The first issue was a modest one, only nineteen pages, written and edited by Maximilian himself with a printing of five thousand copies. It was called *The Knight*. The magazine was well-received, but with the failing economy, paper and printing costs threatened its continuation. Maximilian realized that he would have to buy a press and print it himself. Knowing that many of his community members in Kraków were suspicious of his work, starting a printing house there would not work. His best option seemed to be an unused friary in the remote town of

Grodno in northeast Poland. He bought an antiquated press, was able to get some money, persuaded a few friars from the Order to join him, and got down to business.

The friars worked long hours, cranking the press by hand. Gradually the publication took off, from 12,000 the first year to 70,000 copies three years later. They were able to buy more modern machines and were able to recruit more young friars, so that by 1927 twenty-two brothers were working in Maximilian's print shop. But as in Kraków, the older members of the community became disgruntled with all the fervor of Maximilian and his young followers and the situation became increasingly strained for him.

At the same time, Maximilian's health began to fail again. Overworked and anxious about the tension in his community, he had a tubercular relapse and had to be placed once again in a sanatorium. From there he continued to assist with the magazine through correspondence.

Once Kolbe had recuperated, he returned to work at the press in Grodno. He had lost his head printer to typhus and other friars were becoming infected with tuberculosis. He realized that his publishing had outgrown the cramped and unhealthy quarters in the friary and it was time to move on. In 1927 Kolbe was given a large tract of land near Warsaw. He had his printing presses shipped there and, with the help of some of his fellow friars, began building simple wooden structures that would serve as a monastery and print shop.

By 1929 the magazine's circulation reached 100,000 and Kolbe was also printing religious books and pamphlets that circulated throughout Poland. More young people were attracted to the monastery and within two years there were sixty-seven brothers and candidates and thirty-three young seminarians.

Spreading the Mission to Asia

Now that Kolbe's printing center was successful, he turned his eyes to the Asian missions. In 1930 he went to Rome for permission and then booked passage for Shanghai for himself and four other friars, none of whom had any language or cultural preparation.

Kolbe and his friars were welcomed in Korea and then China and the prospects for printing *The Knight* seemed favorable. Gradually, Maximilian began to realize that the various groups of European missionaries protected their own turf. Distributing his magazine was not a problem, but he could not print it in China. Kolbe then decided to try Japan and headed for Nagasaki, which had a large Catholic community. Kolbe was greeted warmly by the local bishop, who needed a professor of philosophy in his seminary. Kolbe agreed to take on the position and teach philosophy in Latin, if he could publish his magazine. He also wrote his magazine articles in Latin and had them translated into Japanese. Amazingly, one month to the day of his arrival he was able to publish 10,000 copies of the first *Knight* in Japanese.

Maximilian left Japan for the last time in 1936 to return to Poland. The mission in Japan had its setbacks but continued to grow and, amazingly, survived the war. The mission struggled during the war and when the atomic bomb was dropped on Nagasaki in August, 1945 it was one of the few buildings left standing. Maximilian's Japanese mission brought in those horribly burned by radiation and nursed them. Many children who had been orphaned were also given shelter and care by the Franciscans.

Return to Poland

By the time Maximilian returned to the friary he had established near Warsaw, it had become a small town with over eight hundred members. The presses were humming with eleven different publications, and the friary had its own radio station. Subscriptions to *The Knight* were climbing toward a million copies, and Maximilian's militia numbered nearly 700,000 in Poland and hundreds of thousands in other parts of the world.[6]

Kolbe served as superior of the community and was constantly available to support and encourage his friars. Those who knew him often commented on his extraordinary holiness, his love of fun and laughter, his deep commitment to prayer, and the warmth and friendship he shared with all the members of the community. One said that he was a great leader, not because he was a good orator or because he was an intellectual, but rather because he knew how to inspire.[7]

When Maximilian returned to Poland, Adolf Hitler was Fuhrer of Germany and was mobilizing for the building of his empire. At the same time, Kolbe was mobilizing his spiritual army to take on the force of the Blitzkrieg. The power of love and mercy would stand against the power of hatred and destruction. Later on all this would take on real flesh and blood when Maximilian faced the horrors of the death camps.

The Invasion of Poland

In 1939 Hitler invaded Poland, crushing any resistance. Kolbe's friary with its extensive publishing operation and radio station, which had been critical of German aggression and atrocities, was shut down.[8] Kolbe had wisely sent his friars home beforehand, telling them in his farewell that he would not survive the war. His final words to his followers were: "Do not forget love!"[9]

Soon after the invasion, Kolbe was arrested by the Gestapo, taken to a prison in Warsaw and then shipped on a five-day trip in a cattle car to an internment camp at Amitz, across the German border. After being transferred to several other prisons, Maximilian was released and allowed to return to his monastery. Seemingly, he and many others considered to be troublemakers and leaders were given a taste of the harsh realities of concentration camp life to discourage them from any future resistance. If they persisted in threatening the reich, the next time would be the real thing. In the meantime, the Nazis were still formulating plans to exterminate those whom they perceived to be their enemies, including those who were considered to be too inferior to be part of the thousand-year reich.

After three months Kolbe returned to his monastery, only to find a few ancient printing machines were left of Kolbe's vast printing operation. Still, the indefatigable Kolbe immediately began restoration. Amazingly, he even applied to the Gestapo to begin publishing again, assuring them that his magazine would only preach the service of love and would avoid politics.

The Monastery Becomes a Refuge
While hoping for permission to publish again, Kolbe transformed his friary into a care center for the many refugees of the war. He set up a hospital, a pharmacy, and repair shops for clothing and shoes. The kitchen and bakery provided three meals a day for fifteen hundred local refugees, who lived in severe deprivation and fear. By 1940, Kolbe was leading a center that served thirty-five hundred refugees, including fifteen hundred Jews, while suffering in his sickbed from bouts of TB.

Apparently, imprisonment had not taught Maximilian his lesson. As one author puts it: "Silence him, and his generous hands would say what his mouth could no longer say. Forbid him to express his faith; he would cultivate hope; and the charity that had come through his writings now came through his hospital."[10]

Maximilian must have been as surprised as anyone when he was given permission to publish one more issue of his magazine. Predictably, he put the edition out on December 8, the Feast of the Immaculate Conception, and wrote three pieces himself. One was on the purpose of the magazine, another praising Mary, and a final coded article on "The Truth."

Not showing his hand as to what the "Truth" was, Kolbe said that it was so powerful that it can never be effectively overcome by contradictors. This Truth cannot be changed. It can be sought after, found, recognized. We can conform our lives to it and build our happiness on it.[11] The Nazis, caught up in so many lies and perversions, must have been able to read between the lines. This was Kolbe's last article.

Dark Clouds
Spies and informers were sent to Kolbe's friary and dutifully denounced the center as one of "resistance." One last effort was made to get the bright and energetic leader Kolbe to come over to the Nazi side. Given

his German-sounding name, he was offered German citizenship so that his talents could be used to support the Nazis. Kolbe sealed his fate by turning down the offer, and knew that his days were numbered. In February 1941 Hitler invaded Russia. Not wanting any possibility of Polish resistance, Hitler ordered massive arrests and deportations. The "inferior" Slavic, Polish peasants were to be left, without the guidance of their beloved priests and intellectual leaders, to till the soil and provide food for the "master race." Any troublemakers were to be eliminated. In less than a year, the Nazis formulated their Final Solution, wherein 6 million Jews and other "enemies" and "inferiors" would be systematically gassed and cremated in concentration camps.

The Arrest

Kolbe received a tip that he was going to be arrested on February 17. The night before has been compared to Jesus' own Last Supper. Kolbe gathered several of his friars to share a cake and told them that the prospect of being able to shed his blood for his ideals gave him an inner joy. During the night he got up several times and asked friends to pray with him for strength. At daybreak Maximilian rose, put on his best habit and waited until the dreaded black cars pulled into the driveway. He greeted the police with the Franciscan "Praised be Jesus Christ" and was then put into a car with four other friars and taken to the Pawiak prison in Warsaw.

Pawiak Prison

In Pawiak prison Kolbe was beaten repeatedly for his faith. Edward Gniadek, an eyewitness, recounts one story. He tells how an SS guard pulled Kolbe's crucifix and asked: "Do you believe?" When Kolbe answered "Yes" he was punched in the face. He was asked the same question repeatedly and gave the same answer. Kolbe was beaten until the guard gave up and marched out of the room in frustration.[12]

Maximilian was able to write several letters back to his friary. These letters do not comment on his suffering, but are filled with hope, concern for the health of his brothers, and encouragement to be strong and prayerful. He does tell them at one point that he has been down with a high fever and he requests warm work clothes. The letters are filled with cordial greetings, blessings, and love. They are signed *Raymond Kolbe* since he can no longer sign himself as a Franciscan priest.[13] At one point, twenty of his young friars courageously asked the Gestapo that they be allowed to accept the charges against Kolbe and take his place in prison. The Gestapo turned down the offer, but it provides an example of how well he had taught his brothers the lesson of heroism and love. The incident also provides insight into why he was so willing to offer his own life for another in the death camp.

The Death Camp
After three months in Pawiak prison, Kolbe was shipped to the infamous concentration camp Auschwitz.

The French writer and former prisoner himself, Andre Frossard, offers a reflection on this hellhole:

> I come now to the unthinkable and the unforgiveable, to the suffering of the innocent, to the far-off sobs of mothers carried away by a storm of grief, those hills of shoes removed from children were a smile and then soot. I come to speak of Auschwitz, the damp plain with indefinite boundaries, where the earth evaporates, where the fog draws its shrouds over the memory of those poor beings who tried in vain to protect with fleshless hands their last spark of life, breathing more and more feebly the poisoned air filled with lethal fumes and the last gasps of the dead.[14]

When Kolbe arrived at Auschwitz, the camp was still a work in progress. It had been an old Polish army camp, now converted into a prison and work camp. Torture chambers had been set up in the basement, firing squad walls had been built, gassing was being experimented with, and some cremation ovens had been constructed. It would be some time before a massive camp would be built nearby consisting of a long series of stables for the prisoners, massive gas chambers, and rows of ovens.

Only then could thousands of victims be shipped in and several thousand killed and burned in industrial fashion each day.

Kolbe was greeted at the camp by Commander Karl Fritsch, who spoke with a scoffing tone of ridicule: "You have come here, not to a sanatorium,…but to a German concentration camp from which there is just one exit, the crematory chimney. If that displeases you, you can leave at once by the high tension wires. Now if in this transport there are Jews, they have no right to live longer than two weeks; priests one month, others three months."[15] Typically, the Nazis tried to strip Maximilian of his identity as a person, as well as a Franciscan priest by shaving his head, cutting off his beard, tattooing the number 16670 on his arm, and dressing him in a filthy, striped outfit. In spite of these efforts, many of the prisoners still knew who he was, if not by reputation, by the way he ministered to them secretly in the yards or in the barracks during the night. He often gave his own food to someone whom he thought needed it more than he. He gave away clothing and even his shoes. In the evenings Kolbe would lead prayer sessions in the barracks, and he would regularly crawl from bed to bed to comfort the other prisoners, show them compassion, and keep up their spirits. Taking the drafty bed by the door, he would greet with a smile those entering and bless the sick and dying being carried out. In the hollow eyes, the deeply lined face, the stick-like body, they could see the spirit of Maximilian shining brightly. There was an urgency to Kolbe's life now. It was as though he was trying to use every minute left to him to teach the power of love, forgiveness, and mercy. One physician who was with Kolbe has written: "His reflections on the mercy of God went straight to my heart. His words to forgive the persecutors and to overcome evil with good, kept me from collapsing into despair."[16]

Even though Kolbe was seriously ill with tuberculosis, often burning up with fever, he was assigned to work crews. They made him haul huge carts of gravel to build the crematorium walls. They assigned him to haul corpses to the ovens. They mocked him, beat him, and set dogs on him. But there was no way they could get to that inner peace and love in Maximilian's heart. A fellow prisoner, who survived, remembers Kolbe saying:

> No, no,…these Nazis will not kill our souls, since we prisoners certainly distinguish ourselves quite definitely from our tormentors. They will not be able to deprive us of the dignity of our Catholic belief. We will not give up. And when we die, then we die pure and peaceful, resigned to God in our hearts.[17]

He wrote to his mother: "I am faring well. Be calm, Mother, and don't worry about me or my health. God is everywhere, who watches over all and everything with great love."[18]

The camp had changed Kolbe. No longer was he driven to spread his devotions or convert the world. It was as though he was now able to transcend his Polish spirituality and Catholic faith. He was now able to go beyond nationality and religion and simply reach out to the suffering with gentleness and compassion. His identity now "anchors him all the more firmly in the human family, his priesthood means total openness to the needs of others."[19]

Kolbe Steps Out for Another

It was not easy to escape Auschwitz. There were highly charged electric fences around the camp, watchtowers from which guards would shoot anyone moving away from the path, and sirens that would warn external guards of any movement outside the camp. The one way someone could escape was to go outside the camp in a work crew and make a mad dash for freedom. However, there was a policy to deter such events.

On the last day of July, 1941, the scream of the sirens signaled an escape, and the horrid drill of stand-out began.

Once the escapees were not found, ten were selected for the Death Block. Kolbe stepped up and took another's place.

The End

We would have no idea what happened to Maximilian once he entered the Death Block had it not been for the testimony of a Polish prisoner who worked there as a secretary and translator. He tells the story of how the ten men were stripped naked and hurled into a cell where they would receive no food or water until they died. Every day the guards entered the cell and gave orders for the dead to be dragged out. The prisoners often cried out for food or drink but were pushed aside. Anyone who rushed for the door was kicked to the floor and shot. The bucket which was left for their waste was usually dry, showing that the prisoners were so desperate that they drank their own urine.

In spite of the unspeakable suffering in the death cell, our witness says that Maximilian kept up the spirits of the prisoners by leading them in the rosary and in singing. The witness testifies: "Father Maximilian Kolbe of blessed memory bore himself like a hero. He made no requests and no complaints. He gave courage to the others and encouraged them to hope that the fugitive would be found and they would be released."[20] Even the guards were amazed at Kolbe's strength and commented that they had never seen a prisoner like him.

After two weeks, only five of the ten prisoners were alive and the cell was needed for other prisoners. It was decided to inject poison into their arms to kill them.

Our witness tells us that Kolbe raised his arm with a prayer on his lips and then sank back against the wall, his face "serene and beautiful and radiant."[21] His body was placed in a wooden box and taken to the crematorium to be incinerated. It was the Feast of the Assumption.

A Modern Saint

Maximilian Kolbe was beatified in 1971 by Paul VI and canonized in 1982 by John Paul II, who, like Kolbe suffered under the Nazi occupation of Poland, and who often visited the cell where his hero was tortured and killed. John Paul II shared Kolbe's Polish devotion to Mary, his courage to stand up to violent oppressors with the power of love and truth. He shared his passion to use the media to communicate the gospel of justice and peace to the world.

Maximilian is a hero of peace because he demonstrated throughout his life and most profoundly in his death that love is stronger than hatred and violence and will ultimately defeat such evils. He is a hero of justice, not in any juridical sense, but in the biblical sense of fidelity to the highest law, the law of love. His following of Jesus exposed the hypocrisies of his age and taught the justice of the beatitudes. He was indeed a just man, a man of holiness whose life stands as a beacon in one of the darkest times of human history.

Kolbe offers us a unique theology of justice, seeing justice as holiness, righteousness, holding the love of God and neighbor in balance. He offers us a theology of peace which goes beyond the lack of war and conquest. His is inner peace which comes from compassion and being able to suffer for and with others. It is a peace that comes from not clinging to the things of life or even to life itself, a letting go to the care of God that gives one strength. Kolbe's spirit was indomitable and simply could not be broken even by torture and deprivation.

chapter seven

Cardinal Joseph Bernardin

The cardinal's body had been brought to his house for viewing by the family and friends. Soon after, the funeral cortege moved down Chicago's State Street, which was lined with mourners all the way to the cathedral. For forty-one hours people of all ages and faiths came four abreast to pay their respects to Joseph, who often described himself as their "brother." A Mass followed, celebrated by dignitaries and the folk, blending together as a family around their loved one. His driver, Monsignor Kenneth Velo, gave a rousing tribute to the cardinal and ended with the words Joseph so liked to hear after being out visiting his people: "Cardinal Eminence, You're home. You're home."[1]

Early Years
Joseph Bernardin was born in 1928 in Columbia, South Carolina, the son of two Italian immigrants, "Beppi" and Maria. He was a child of the Great Depression and would be frugal all his life. His father died when Joseph was only six years old, requiring him to look after his little sister, Elaine, and assume the cooking and cleaning in public housing while his mother worked long hours as a seamstress.

Joseph's Italian parents passed their Mediterranean temperament to Joseph, so he was hard-working, passionate, and yet able to deal with crises with an inner calm, personal warmth, and tenacity. His cultural background also gave Joseph his strong values of belonging, family, and honor, all of which he transposed into his notion of church.[2]

The compassionate side of Joseph's nature moved him toward medical school, but after one year he decided that he was called instead to the Catholic priesthood. Joseph entered the seminary as part of the wave that swept into the seminaries during the boom of the forties and fifties. Church life was a good fit for him and he pursued his studies diligently and earned the degrees necessary to be ordained in 1952. He received a master's in education the same year.

For the next fourteen years, Bernardin was a dutiful church clerk, serving various bishops of his diocese in official capacities. Later he would characterize himself as typical of many of the young clergy of that period: "You just did what you were supposed to in those days—go where they sent you, do what they asked of you."[3]

Joseph was a southerner and was neither Irish nor trained in Rome, and hardly had the résumé for a successful member of the hierarchy at the time. It was Bernardin's intelligence and diligence that kept him on a straight track up the ecclesiastical ladder.[4] At age thirty-eight he became the youngest bishop in the United States when he was appointed auxiliary bishop of Atlanta in 1966.

Joseph was taken under the wing of the great archbishop of Atlanta, Paul Hallinan. He was a hard-nosed chaplain during World War II and was to be an important mentor for Joseph. He helped Bernardin get out of his church bubble and become concerned about social justice. Hallinan had a passion for civil rights. He desegregated the Catholic schools of Atlanta, sent priests and nuns into the marches in Selma and Montgomery, and urged the populace to integrate their neighborhoods.

The archbishop was also present and active at the Second Vatican Council and drew Joseph into renewal of the church after the Council. He appointed many laypeople to positions in the diocese and taught Joseph the importance of consultation, collaboration, and mediation. He helped prepare Joseph to be a post–Vatican II bishop, one who was not simply a messenger of the Vatican, but a pastoral leader in this own right. Hallinan taught him to be patient, to keep the long view of things, and to never panic under pressure. He helped shape Joseph to be a bishop who was both loyal to the church and sensitive to people's needs.[5] Sadly, the archbishop became so ill that he had to depend more and more on Joseph until his death at fifty-seven.

The National Conference of Catholic Bishops
In 1968 Bernardin came on to the national scene as he assumed the role of general secretary of the bishops' conference. He had already achieved a reputation of being pastorally and politically savvy. [6] The days of each bishop working independently in his own fiefdom were coming to an end during the crucial years after Vatican II, and the bishops were learning how to work together as a group and find their voices on public issues in the modern world. Bernardin held this post for four years.

These were troubled times, with violent riots in the cities, civil rights marches, war protests, Lyndon Johnson's refusal to run for another term, and the assassinations of Martin Luther King, Jr., and Robert Kennedy. The bishops were being called upon to use their new powers to work collaboratively and take positions not only on church issues but on issues pertinent to the church's role in the modern world. Down the line they would have to enter such unfamiliar areas as economics and nuclear power.

Bernardin worked well with the other bishops and helped shape the conference into a force in the American Catholic church. It was under his guidance that the Campaign for Human Development was shaped, giving money to programs assisting the poor. He was often called in to mediate between rebellious priests and their bishops, especially during the controversy over *Humanae Vitae*, and his prudence and wisdom in these matters gained him trust among the bishops as well as in the Vatican.

In his work with the bishops in Washington, D.C., Bernardin came under the tutelage of another great American church leader, John Dearden. The bishop was his former biblical professor and had been known as "Iron John" because of his firm hand in authoritative matters.

But Vatican II had brought about a profound conversion in Dearden, and as bishop of Detroit he worked tirelessly to promote the new image of the church as "the people of God." He gave his people a vested interest in their church, listened to their views and worked collaboratively with them to make the Vatican II renewal a reality. It was Dearden who organized the first Call to Action Conference in Detroit and thus began a movement that, though controversial, still actively promotes the progressive agenda in the American church. Archbishop Dearden became a role model for this renewal and deeply affected his understudy, Joseph. He also saw to it that his younger protégé was introduced to the movers and shakers in the Vatican. He taught him to stand confidently among his peers and to never panic during stormy times.

Cincinnati

In 1972 Bernardin was warmly welcomed as the new archbishop of Cincinnati. He came into office with such purpose and open communication that the people soon realized that they had an extraordinary and experienced leader, one who was well thought of both among the American hierarchy and at the Vatican.

In his first Christmas sermon, Bernardin called for peace in Vietnam, clearly indicating that he would be an active player in the large issues facing the church in this country. He then proceeded to build upon the Vatican II renewal that had been accomplished by his predecessor, Archbishop Paul Francis Liebold. With the eye of an experienced and professional organizer, he put the diocesan structures in good order. He moved out of the bishop's residence to an apartment in a diocesan property and streamlined and centralized the diocesan offices. At the same time, Bernardin gained a reputation throughout the diocese for being consultative and collaborative. For Joseph, everyone's opinion mattered and he liked to hear all sides of a situation before coming to a considered decision.[7] He graciously accepted the vision that the people of the diocese had already formulated, but at the same time he wanted to put his own stamp on it. Ever the pastor, Joseph regularly visited the parishes, nursing homes, and prisons. The small-town spirit of the Cincinnati folk deeply affected Joseph and it was here that he developed his strong people skills. [8]

The bishop's national stature became apparent when he was asked to preach at a service in the White House following Nixon's second inauguration. Once again, Bernardin demonstrated that he was not merely interested in pious sayings, but was concerned with linking the gospel with the modern world. In his sermon he challenged Nixon's stance on rugged individualism, pointing out that such emphasis can lead to selfish interests that ignore concerns for others and the common good. Joseph was not trying to be "a skunk at the garden party," but he did want to make it clear that both he and the church had strong positions on social justice.

The Cincinnatians received further indication that their archbishop had national influence when he was elected president of the bishops' conference in 1974. It was a stormy time in the American church, with a great division between progressives and traditionalists, many priests, brothers, and nuns leaving, and many Catholics turning to their consciences for moral decisions rather than the official teachings of the church. At the same time, the national scene was disturbed over Watergate and the eventual resignation of the president. The bishops wanted a clear thinker and calm hand at the tiller and they knew that Bernardin was such a person.

During his tenure, Bernardin had to face the controversies swirling around the recent *Roe v. Wade* decision on abortion. Even then, however, he began to insist that the abortion issue be related to other pro-life issues. He also had to stand amid the controversies over such issues as celibacy and the ordination of women precipitated by his former mentor, Cardinal Dearden, with his Call to Action conference. While he did not repudiate the conference he felt that many of its recommendations were premature and inopportune. In addition, Bernardin had to delicately deal with the Vatican's objections to American procedures for granting annulments, procedures which Rome thought too liberal.

Joseph also worked with the apostolic delegate, Jean Jadot, who initiated a progressive process of consulting the laity and clergy in each diocese that needed a new bishop. The process resulted in the refreshing appointment of some young progressive and social justice-minded bishops in some dioceses throughout the United States. Unfortunately, this process was short-lived and the selection of bishops returned to the secretive one that had prevailed before Jadot.

A Point of Conversion

During his tenure in Cincinnati, Bernardin reached a turning point in his life. He recalled that for his first twenty years as a priest he had given a higher priority to good works over prayer. He began to feel hypocritical in urging others to pray when he was not giving enough time to it himself.

One evening he was having dinner with three of his younger priests when he told them that he was having difficulty praying and asked for their help. The priests were blunt in their answer. Here he was a bishop urging others to pray when he was not praying sufficiently! They urged him to set aside time for personal prayer. Bernardin heeded their advice and decided to always give the first hour of his day to prayer and meditation. He found that this opened his life wider to God. He writes: "This put my life in a new and uplifting perspective; I also found that I was able to share the struggles of my own spiritual journey with others. Knowing that I went through the same things they did gave them great encouragement."[9] Prayer gave him the inner peace and strength to weather the storms ahead when he would be falsely accused of sexual misconduct and then diagnosed with cancer.

Chicago

In 1983 Bernardin was raised to the summit of his ecclesiastical career when he was appointed head of the Archdiocese of Chicago. Here he succeeded the embattled Cardinal John Cody, who systematically had lost the support of many of the members of the archdiocese and clergy through mismanagement, heavy-handedness, and an increasingly reclusive lifestyle.

Bernardin took over a church that was dispirited and chaotic and, with his quiet, efficient, and pastoral approach, the healing began. He addressed a suspicious clergy at his first conference with the affectionate and disarming words from Scripture: "I am Joseph, your brother."[10] This would be his mantra for the next thirteen years through stormy disputes over parish and school closings, sex-abuse scandals, false charges against himself, the loss of over three-hundred resigned priests. Always maintaining his own dignity and honoring the dignity of others, he weathered the stormy controversies over pastoral ministry to gay and lesbian Catholics, serving AIDS victims, liturgical practices such as communal penance, and medical ethics in the Catholic hospitals. His chief skill seemed to be his ability to listen, and he would patiently hear all sides before coming to a decision. Common ground and consensus were the watchwords of his managerial style. His open transparency with the press stood in stark contrast to the evasiveness and secrecy they had experienced in the past.

The New Challenge of Peace
A few months after Bernardin arrived in Chicago, the United States Conference of Catholic Bishops (USCCB) published their powerful pastoral letter on peace, *Peacemaking: Moral and Policy Challenges for a New World*. Bernardin had worked very hard as the chairman of the committee that produced this historic document. The motivations were in part to apply papal teachings, especially those of John Paul II on war and peace, to nuclear policies of the United States. The bishops also wanted to broaden their concern for human life beyond the abortion question, to call for a redirection of global resources away from instruments of destruction, to satisfy the human needs of the poor, and to provide a clear moral voice to the arms race.[11]

Peacemaking was a new kind of church document. Rather than speaking from church authority alone, it spoke from years of consultation with experts in many fields, scientific, political, military, financial, as well as theological. For the first nine months many witnesses were called, including senior officials from the United States government. Always committed to consultation and consensus, Bernardin circulated the first draft to the episcopal conferences of other countries and to Rome for comments and suggestions. A second draft was then circulated and hundreds of amendments were considered. The bishops received an extensive commentary from the Reagan Administration, especially on the bishops' criticism of American policy. Finally, a fine-tuned third draft was submitted to the bishops for amendments and a final vote of approval.

The process, led by Bernardin, was a classic post–Vatican II approach. The bishops had taken seriously their new collegial powers, were reading the "signs of the times," and were not only addressing the modern world, but letting the modern world shape their perspectives. Bernardin had spent many years helping to shape the American bishops' conference into a powerful collegial body and now this conference was speaking with a strong authority, based on collaboration and consultation with both church and state.

A Summary

The Challenge of Peace is devoted to the prospect of constructing peace in an interdependent world. It sees the nuclear question in the context of human rights, justice, and the rights of all nations. Its primary focus is the prevention of the use of nuclear weapons and the limitation of other uses of force. The context is Catholic teaching on the duty of the state to defend society, the state's right to use force as a last resort, and the need for moral criteria when force is used.[12]

In Bernardin's commentary on the document, he points out that the bishops recognize that the use of nuclear weapons is a qualitatively new moral problem, one that goes beyond any earlier questions of warfare. This is a revolutionary challenge and the bishops are skeptical as to whether nuclear weapons can be used in a controlled way.[13]

Bernardin discusses three "cases" raised by the bishops. The first is "counter-population" warfare or attacks on civilian centers, which they cannot ever justify, even when our own cities are attacked. The second is the "initiation of nuclear war," which the bishops cannot see as morally justified. The third case is "limited nuclear war." Here the bishops maintain that the entire burden of proof rests on those who maintain that limited use can be done within moral limits. The bishops are once again skeptical that such proof can be put forward. As for using nuclear weapons for deterrence, the bishops maintain a strictly conditioned moral acceptance, saying: "Only if deterrence is a transitional strategy." Their main intent is to call for aggressive arms control, disarmament of nuclear systems.

The bishops' peace document made a profound impact on the Catholic mentality on the nuclear question. It also made those in government aware that the bishops of this country were able to speak with an authority gained not only from their own church positions, but also from an extended dialogue with experts. Bernardin had built new bridges between church and state in this country and gave the bishops a new voice.

The document was so significant that it shook the Reagan White House, which was planning for a strong military buildup. It also raised the eyebrows of some in the Vatican, who feared that the American bishops' heads were perhaps getting too big for their miters and that they were becoming too strong a voice on international matters. It is significant that just one year after the peace document was issued, Cardinal Joseph Ratzinger, prefect of the Congregation for the Doctrine of the Faith, declared that bishops' conferences did not have any magisterial or teaching function.[14] In 1993 John Paul II issued a directive that all bishops conferences had to send their pastoral letters to Rome for approval. Since then, the American bishops seem to have lost the powerful collegial voice they had gained at Vatican II.

New Signs of the Times
After the collapse of the Soviet Union in 1991, Bernardin noted that the nuclear question had shifted. With the Cold War over, the fear of the clash of the superpowers ended, but now there were new concerns over other ethnic and national struggles. The threat of nuclear war was replaced with the threat of nuclear proliferation. Isolationism and indifference to the poor had worsened the situation, while human rights abuses and atrocities had become more widespread.

Bernardin maintained that peacemaking called for the United States to help build an international order in service of the common good.[15] He called for the construction of a political ethic in United States foreign policy. This should include a moral vision of peace and justice wherein Americans saw themselves as part of the human family and were concerned about every suffering member. This new vision would include the guarding of human rights and service to the oppressed throughout the world. It would promote an international order and address inequities among nations. He urged the United States to rediscover its best values of justice and freedom so that it could be an example for the world. He concluded: "What the United States can offer the world—and what the world desperately needs—is creative engagement, a willingness to collaborate, and a commitment to values that can build up the global community through an ethic of cooperative security."[16]

The Seamless Garment
Bernardin's concerns over the massive destruction of human life that could be brought about by nuclear war brought him to broader considerations about the value of life. He began to point out that billions were being spent on armaments in a world where many live in grinding poverty. In 1983, in a speech on Martin Luther King, Jr., he agreed with the civil rights leader that "peace is the fruit of justice."[17] He pointed out that true peace cannot exist within nations or among nations unless the claims of justice by people are acknowledged. King had pointed out that peace in this country was precarious and unstable, because the full

human and civil rights of many were not being recognized. Bernardin observed that too often we engage in war to gain peace, when in fact the effective approach is to build a peace where war is unnecessary. He confronted the notion that we can't be secure with millions spent on the military, while countless are starving and dying in poverty. To his fellow Americans, he challenged: "What view of security moves us as a nation to believe that hungry and homeless people in the world's wealthiest democracy is a basis for a stable domestic peace?"[18]

Bernardin insisted that all human life is sacred and that we have the responsibility to preserve and protect it. Technological advances have extended what we can do and made the questions surrounding what we ought to do more complex. For Bernardin, respect for life means for *all* life and therefore focuses not only on war and abortion, but also areas such as capital punishment, and care for the terminally ill. Our moral responsibilities do not stop at the moment of birth. Moreover, the right to life is linked with the quality of life. As Bernardin puts it: "Those who defend the right to life of the weakest among us must be equally visible in support to the quality of life of the powerless among us: the old and the young, the hungry and the homeless, the undocumented immigrant and the unemployed worker."[19]

To answer those who objected that this seamless approach would smother Catholic opposition to abortion and the arms race, Bernardin maintained that each moral issue has its own meaning and morality. He was adamant that the consistent ethic of life does not collapse all life issues into one problem. Each life issue must be seen as a piece of a larger picture.[20] The larger pattern is one of the sacredness of all life, whether it is the life of a fetus, an enemy soldier, a condemned inmate, or a terminally ill person. His intent was to develop a systemic vision of Catholic ethics, within which specific positions can be taken on a whole range of issues. He did not want to equate the taking of innocent life with the taking of a condemned criminal or with the preserving of life with good health care. What Bernardin wanted to do was view the protection and promotion of all human life as a moral question. The moral situations are by no means to be equated (unborn life and the life of a murderer), but they are to be seen as related because both involve the taking of a human life.[21]

Bernardin constantly extended his consistent ethic of life approach. He was strongly opposed to capital punishment. He believed that the desire to see criminals executed often arose out of revenge and was not compatible with the gospel teaching of forgiveness and reconciliation. He writes: "Capital punishment, to my mind, is an example of meeting violence with violence. What does that say about the quality of our life when people celebrate the death of another human being?"[22]

Bernardin's visits to Auschwitz moved him deeply to oppose anti-Semitism and the horrific loss of life it brought about in the Holocaust. Bernardin was dedicated to dialogue with his Jewish sisters and brothers. He wrote: "Never again can we permit ourselves to be alienated from each other; never again can we let our minds and hearts be misshaped by the prejudices and hatreds of the past."[23]

At the same time he was candid in his criticisms of Jewish extremists in Israel and their abuse of Palestinians.[24] Bernardin was also aware of the environmental crisis and spoke out against the damage to the human family. He wrote: "Never before in the history of civilization have men and women needed to be concerned about the survival of the natural world on which we are increasingly recognizing our dependence."[25]

Dealing With an Unjust Accusation
In November of 1993 Bernardin faced one of the most devastating challenges of his life—he was publicly accused of sexually abusing a seminarian while he was archbishop of Cincinnati. A lawsuit had been filed in Cincinnati by Steven Cook and the allegations were released to the press. Given the climate of the time with allegations being made against numerous priests, many people were disposed to believe the charges.

The irony here is that in 1985 Bernardin had unsuccessfully asked the American bishops to study the question of priests sexually abusing children. Early in 1993 he had put in place excellent policies and procedures in his own Archdiocese for dealing with such cases. He now submitted his own case to the Board that dealt with these matters. Bernardin says that he felt disgraced and humiliated, as though he was in the presence of evil itself. The words of Jesus calmed him: "The truth will set you free (Jn 8:32)."[26] He then gave a written statement to the reporters saying: "I have never abused anyone in all my life, anywhere, any time, any place."[27] Bolstered by prayer and the many letters and calls of support, including one from the Holy See, Bernardin held a press conference with nearly seventy reporters and simply told them that he was innocent of the charges and had always led a chaste and celibate life. The tension in the room subsided and it seemed that the reporters were beginning to believe him. In the fourteen grueling press conferences that followed, the same process was followed and Bernardin came to feel some relief.

Within several months the charges against Bernardin were declared false. The evidence collapsed and it was revealed that Cook had been drawn into a conspiracy hatched by some of Bernardin's enemies. Cook dropped the charges. In a later conciliatory meeting with Bernardin, the young man declared that he was never abused by the bishop and apologized for saying that he was. The two men were reconciled. Bernardin gave the young man a Bible, celebrated a Mass with him, and then anointed him with the sacrament of the sick. Cook, who was seriously ill with AIDS, died later that year.

One Cross After Another

Joseph began 1995 as a new man, freed from the burden of false charges and ready to work with vigor and hope. He made three international trips to have meetings on such topics as child pornography, the church and young people, and Jewish-Catholic dialogue. He returned in high spirits and took on the work of the diocese with intense enthusiasm.

Then suddenly another major setback occurred. After some lab tests he was told that he had pancreatic cancer and needed surgery. Wanting to be completely transparent with his people, Joseph called a press conference and revealed his diagnosis.

During his time in the hospital for chemotherapy treatments, Joseph grew close to other cancer patients, including small children. (One little girl called him "The Pope Man"). He was now not only their priest, but also a fellow patient in solidarity with them through his own cancer. He wrote:

> In the light of my cancer ministry, I began to recognize the unique and special nature of another community to which I now belong: the community of those who suffer from cancer and other serious illnesses. Those in this community see things differently. Life takes on new meaning, and suddenly it becomes easier to separate the essential from the peripheral.[28]

He wanted the patients to know that he walked with them as their brother and their friend.

When his cancer went into remission, Bernardin was able to continue his work in the archdiocese. He now had a special dedication to Catholic health care and both wrote and lectured on the subject. One of his favorite ministries was with young adults and he would host them with a picnic on his lawn when their lecture series Theology on Tap was completed. However, Joseph suffered a series of falls from spinal problems and osteoporosis, fracturing several vertebrae and ribs, and requiring back surgery. In early August, 1996, Bernardin rejoiced in being cancer-free for the fifteen months since his original surgery.

The Common Ground Project

Before his spinal surgery, Bernardin prepared for a conference dedicated to bringing the various divided factions of the American Catholic church together for peaceful dialogue. He believed that the polarization and mean-spiritedness in the church was threatening its unity, undermining the Vatican II renewal, and blocking fresh thinking about the future. On a personal note, he said that his battle with cancer had altered his perspective on life so that what had before seemed important was now trivial. He focused only on the matters that were truly significant. Peace in his church was one of those matters.

Joseph's object was to sponsor conferences that would bring together persons of diverse perspectives and search for what he called Catholic Common Ground.[29] He expected these dialogues to work within the boundaries of church teaching and face the challenges meeting the church and society today.

Bernardin received diverse reactions to his proposal from his fellow bishops. Cardinal Bernard Law of Boston objected that the plan was not very helpful and the dissent just couldn't be dialogued away. Cardinal James Hickey of Washington, D.C., argued that the initiative did not give the magisterium of the church its proper due. At the same time, many in the hierarchy, including Cardinal Roger Mahony of Los Angeles, enthusiastically supported the idea.

Bernardin calmly answered his critics. To those who feared the dialogues would legitimatize dissent, he pointed out that honest dialogue listens, but does not necessarily agree. Moreover, he pointed out that there is often legitimate dissent in the church, which can be the basis for moving forward. And to those who suggested that the centrality of Jesus or the primacy of Scripture and tradition would be compromised by such dialogue, Joseph was adamant that nothing was further from his mind. And to those who objected that this would all lead to heresy, he pointed out that his objective was to stay within the limits of the tradition and yet focus on pastoral issues and explore how the church might best address the gospel to the world.

Joseph did not live to see his dream of Common Ground come to realization. After his death, the first conferences were held and surprisingly there was little controversy. It was concluded that among the high number of participants there was little disagreement. (Those from the far right and far left were not there!) Since then there have been conferences each year, but the movement has not yet had much impact on Catholic life in this country.

The End

In late August, Joseph received word that his cancer had spread to the liver and that he had a year or less to live. Again he called the press, with whom he now had a special bond, and told them the news. There were deep feelings in the room and many were moved to tears as he shared: "As a person of faith, I see death as a friend, as the transition from earthly life to life eternal."[30]

The cardinal continued his work, going to D.C. for a bishops' meeting, visiting the White House where he received the Medal of Freedom, lecturing on the consistent ethic of life and on health care. He went to Rome and visited an ailing pope, made a pilgrimage to Assisi, and then returned to Chicago to deal with diocesan matters and plan his funeral. He visited his beloved mother for the last time in her nursing home, and turned over his authority to an assistant bishop. He was proud to receive the finished copy of his last book, *The Gift of Peace*. Joseph now invited old friends over for a final visit as his health continued to fail. Phone calls came from the president and the pope and at 1:30 AM on a cold November morning, Joseph breathed his last.

Bernardin left a strong legacy of pastoral leadership. His positions on world peace and a consistent life ethic have had a lasting effect in the United States and worldwide. President Barack Obama, in his commencement address at the University of Notre Dame's 2009 graduation, pointed out that he was deeply influenced by Bernardin. While Obama was working as a community organizer in Chicago, he heard the cardinal speak at one of his first meetings as a young lawyer. The president said the cardinal was "a kind and good and wise man. A saintly man," who taught him the value of a consistent ethic of life and the importance of bringing people together to search for common ground.[31]

There is no doubt that Cardinal Joseph Bernardin will live on in the American memory. Joseph was a good man: He was our brother.

chapter eight

Pope John Paul II

Millions of pilgrims, including kings, queens, presidents, prime ministers, cardinals, bishops, and religious leaders from all over the world were gathered for the funeral of one of the best-known figures of the twentieth- and twenty-first centuries, Pope John Paul II. He had burst forth on the world stage in 1978, the first non-Italian pope in four hundred years. Early on the new pontiff was heralded as a linguist, poet, actor, playwright, athlete, and philosopher. Few expected him to become a mystical, iron-willed apostle, who would travel the world as a media superstar and profoundly reshape the religious and political landscape.

There was great emotion and many wept openly during the funeral Mass in the piazza outside St. Peter's, just under the window where John Paul had appeared so often to bless thousands on the square. At the end of the service, attendants picked up his simple wooden coffin and tilted it gently toward the pilgrims. There was suddenly a loud applause, bidding farewell to this beloved servant of Jesus. John Paul's papacy, one of the longest, had come to an end with probably one of the largest gatherings in Christian history.

Early Years

Karol Wojtyla had simple beginnings. He was born on May 18, 1920, in Wadowice, a small town twenty miles south of Kraków, Poland. His father, Karol Wojtyla, Sr., had been a quartermaster in the Polish army.

He was proud to be part of the army, which in 1920 heroically pushed back the Russian army, which outnumbered the Poles three to one, and consequently stopped the spread of Lenin's communist domination. Karol's mother, Emilia, was devout and loving and showered attention on Karol and Edmund, his older brother. Neighbors recall how she would proudly push Karol in his pram and predict that one day he would be a great man.[1]

The family lived in a walk-up three-room flat, owned by a Jewish merchant. Karol, whose nickname was "Lolek," was comfortable with the Jewish community and his best friend was a Jew named Jerzy Kluger, with whom he would keep in touch all his life. His closeness to Jews would be cause for deep grief when he saw so many shipped off to the death camps, and would move him in his papacy to work hard for unity with the Jewish religion.

The parish church and the local Marian shrines, especially Czestochowa, were central in the lives of the Wojtylas. They were inspired by the devoted service of their priests, as well as by the contemplative life of the Carmelite monks who lived in a nearby monastery.

Tragedy seemed to stalk the Wojtyla family. Emilia died when Karol was only nine, and three years later he lost his beloved older brother Edmund, who had often carried him on his shoulders and taught him to ski. Edmund had become a doctor, and died a desolate death from scarlet fever, contracted from a patient. (John Paul II always kept his brother's stethoscope in a drawer of his papal desk.) Karol's experiences with death and loss seemed to bring him even closer to Mary, the mother of Jesus. He turned to her for maternal love and for strength to cope with his suffering.

Father and son were now left alone. Karol's father often became lost in silence and prayer, and though he was a strict disciplinarian, he ruled by example rather than through enforcement. He cooked for his son, played soccer with him in the flat, and even used his tailoring skills to make fine clothes for the boy out of his military uniforms. It was the father who taught Karol to be constantly prayerful. He also filled his son with stories of Poland's proud history and culture and taught him the importance of helping to shape the world around him. At the same time, he allowed young Karol to be a spontaneous lad. He loved to study literature and drama, was quick at sports, and was devoted to serving Mass and singing in the choir, which developed his mellow voice. When Karol was fourteen he met a Polish teacher who ran a youth theater group. Karol had found his passion, acting, where he could get into the skin of another person and relive the great traditions of Poland and Christianity. Early on, he saw how religion, with its great dramatic effect, the great artistic creations of Poland, and the literary classics intersected. Karol was soon to play leading roles in local theaters. Working with attractive leading ladies also gave Karol the opportunity to have close relationships with young women. He had found the world in which he wanted to live. When asked by the local bishop if he wanted to be a priest, Karol said he aspired to be an actor and a poet.

Through acting, Lolek learned the power of the spoken word and gesture. He learned timing, expression, and the power of addressing an audience. He learned lessons that would serve him well when he would assume the role of Christian apostle on the world's stage.

Off to University
When Karol was eighteen, his father moved with him to Kraków, then an intellectual and cultural center, so that the young man could begin studies at the venerable Jagiellonian University. Great thinkers like Copernicus, who discovered that the Earth goes around the sun, had studied in Kraków. Father and son moved into a two-room basement flat, a twenty-minute walk from the center of town and the university. Lolek must have thought himself looking rather bohemian in his black jacket, rough trousers, and black short-visor cap cocked to the side over his rather long blond hair. This was known as the "Slowacki look" after a Polish romantic poet.

POPE JOHN PAUL II

Lolek threw himself into a heavy curriculum of Polish literature and history and continued to write poetry. One poem might have reflected himself at that time, when it referred to "a Slav troubadour." He joined a drama club and continued his spirited performances. One of his favorite roles was Taurus, his birth sign, which describes a personality which is strong, persevering, dominant, obstinate, conservative, and yet healing and soothing. Lolek fit the role!

While Karol and his classmates enjoyed the joys and freedoms of college life, ominous political clouds began to gather in the East. German troops were assembling on the border and there was talk of an invasion. In response students burned effigies of Hitler. It seemed as though young Karol's college career was about to end after just one glorious year.

The War

Karol's life was turned upside down as the Germans crushed the Polish defenses and invaded his country. He and his father gathered their meager belongings and as the "Stukas" bombed and strafed, they fled eastward.

The Germans were ruthless in their efforts to smash the Catholic Polish culture and enslave the people. They massacred women and children, desecrated churches, and rounded up priests for imprisonment. Many young people were shipped off into slave labor. Nazis demolished Polish monuments and libraries, forbade the publication of Polish books and the use of the Polish language in public.

Karol and his father saw many atrocities as they fled to the east. When they heard that the Russians were preparing to invade from that direction, they returned to Kraków. Karol hid in his flat, leaving only for secret lessons in homes until most of his professors were arrested and imprisoned. The theaters were shut down, Mass was forbidden in the Cathedral, and the seminary in Kraków became a garrison for the SS.

Hitler's goal was to destroy Catholic Poland, because he deemed it an inferior culture, dangerous to the Third Reich.

Karol was being tried by fire and his commitment to keep the Catholic Polish culture alive through his acting and poetry galvanized. While working part time for a restaurant, he secretly continued writing plays and poetry that dramatized his struggle and that of his people. In secret meetings in homes, he put on performances with groups who knew discovery would mean immediate arrest and death. At the same time, Karol joined an underground Catholic movement led by a tailor who trained the young students in the mystical writings of John of the Cross and Teresa of Avila and disciplined them in spiritual formation.

To avoid being shipped off as slave labor, Karol got a job mining limestone for a chemical factory. It was cold and grueling work, and his writing reflected a battle with anger and suffering, working as a "robotnik." This experience, as well as his later encounter with priest-workers in France, helped Karol appreciate the lives of workers and later would enable him to address them with empathy as their bishop and pope. He would write an encyclical, On Human Work, celebrating the dignity of work and defending the rights of laborers.

One night, returning from work, Karol found his father dead. The young man was broken, desolate, and now alone in the world. Adding to his despair was the news that the well-known Father Maximilian Kolbe had been killed in nearby Auschwitz. Karol was learning that only the power of Jesus and his Mother could bring light to all this darkness. Later, this would be his message as he traveled a troubled world for decades as pope.

Underground Theater

Karol invited friends from his hometown to join him in the flat in Kraków. Then in a secret meeting a new theater group was formed that would secretly celebrate the Polish culture, preserve the nation's soul and prepare for "its political resurrection" in the future.[2] Simple but powerful performances were carried on in other local flats. And as the Germans became more distracted with the Russian front, the number of performances grew. It was the conviction of the actors that not violence, but truth would bring peace and justice back to their homeland. Truth and beauty would ultimately prevail over evil and hatred! This would be the same formula Karol would use as pope in his struggle to liberate his country from communism.

A Call to the Priesthood

Ultimately, what led Karol to abandon his career in art and join the priesthood was a combination of life-altering events—the death of his father, his commitment to underground Christian communities, his cheating death when he was hit by a truck, and his soul-searching during his reading of various plays. This was not an easy decision, because a youth discovered to be a seminarian could be arrested and shot in Nazi-occupied Poland. The Nazis would eventually kill more than twenty-five thousand priests and five bishops by the war's end.[3] But it was Karol's stubborn commitment to resist the reich with a Catholic Polish determination that carried him through.

The local bishop had set up a system of secret seminary studies, so Karol was able to continue his work in the factory. He took the night shift and in the lulls pursued his study of Thomism, which at first overwhelmed him but then drew him to a lifetime of loyalty. At one point, he attempted to join the Carmelites, but was discouraged by the monks as well as by the bishop. Meanwhile, he continued taking roles in clandestine plays around town. At one point he rescued a young Jewish woman from the Nazis by feeding her and carrying her on his back to the train station.[4] He was also known for his work with the poor in Kraków.[5] Eventually, the Nazis cracked down harder on young people available for slave labor, and Karol had to find refuge in the bishop's house.

When the Nazis were driven out of Poland, they were replaced by the conquering Russians. Catholics were once again allowed to have seminaries, but it was made clear that they either obeyed the communist regime or they would be deported or killed. Karol finished his preparation and was ordained a priest on November 1, 1946. He was then sent to Rome for further study and was mentored by the Dominican Reginald Garrigou-Lagrange. He was a well-known Thomist and expert on John of the Cross, which gave Karol some continuity with his earlier studies. But, Garrigou-Lagrange was also a conservative traditionalist, who contributed to the silencing of priest-scientist Teilhard de Chardin, and to Pius XII's condemnation of the so-called "new theology" that flourished in France in the 1950s. (Much of this theology would later prevail at the Second Vatican Council.)

On his return to Poland, Karol was sent first to a remote country parish, and then transferred to an urban parish in Kraków, where many university students attended. In his new post, he preached to the young and counseled them on sex and marriage, using an approach that would serve as a basis for his later writings in this area. He also took the young people on exciting canoe and hiking trips in the mountains. Karol had discovered his charism with youth, a gift which would become so evident in the enormous youth rallies over which he presided as pope.

Next Karol was sent back to Rome to obtain a doctorate in philosophy, so that he could teach in the university. When he finished his studies, he taught at Lublin University and in the seminary. In 1959 Karol was made auxiliary bishop of Kraków, and then in 1964 was installed as archbishop. He was forty-three years old.

Vatican II

Archbishop Wojtyla was part of the Polish contingent at Vatican II. It is said that he was not comfortable with the open give-and-take among bishops, theologians, and the media. He was more used to a top-down kind of church authority that had become so necessary in the Polish defense of the church against the Nazis and communists. His notion of collegiality was not a forum for shared authority but rather the bishops obeying the pope. This approach would shape the strong and centralized authority he would establish in his papacy and leave him open to the accusation of weakening the authority of local bishops and their conferences. In Catherine Pepinster's *John Paul II* she noted that where

Westerners emphasized the word "team," for John Paul II the word was "captain."[6]

Wojtyla was influential in the Council's statements on marriage and the family and on religious freedom. He was also appointed to the commission that shaped the key document, The Church in the Modern World. But he took a unique slant on this document. Karol agreed that the church must read the "the signs of the times," and he wanted the church to play an active role in world issues. At the same time, he believed, that in his country "openness to the modern world" could be interpreted as giving into the world of fascism or communism. Both were anathema to Wojtyla and as pope he would oppose liberation theology, partially on the grounds that he saw it based on Marxism, which is the basis of communism. Moreover, his Polish experience had taught him that it was unacceptable for priests and bishops to get involved in politics, largely because the politics of the regimes dominating his country were corrupt. Furthermore, it was his experience that those who opposed those regimes usually turned to violence. Later, as pope, these views would influence the way he opposed bishops and priests getting involved in politics in Nicaragua and El Salvador.

After the Vatican Council, Karol was also on the papal commission on birth control and is said to be one of the main drafters of the controversial *Humanae Vitae*, wherein Paul VI forbade artificial contraception.[7] As pope he would vehemently oppose artificial contraception.

The Red Hat

In 1967 Wojtyla was made a cardinal, which gave him considerably more clout in Poland. Over the years there had been constant conflict between church and state, and this new, young cardinal was prepared to take a strong stand for Polish Catholicism and church renewal. He was constantly on the move in his diocese, preaching, teaching, advocating for the building of new churches. He kept pressure on the communist government for religious freedom and strongly resisted repression of any kind. In his sermons, he warned the government that his people are growing in their awareness of human rights.[8] In his pastoral letter, he wrote: "The spirit of freedom is the proper climate for the full development of the person. Without freedom, a person is dwarfed, and all progress dies."[9] Meanwhile, he continued his ministry to young people, taking them hiking, skiing, and entertaining them with his guitar.

An Author

In 1969, Wojtyla published his book *Person and Act*. It is a complicated book, which attempts to integrate Thomism with contemporary philosophy. At the heart of it is Karol's commitment to the dignity of the human person, to personal freedom, and to the solidarity which needs to exist among all persons. He had learned well from the demonic disregard for human life of the Nazis and the denigration of the human person by the communists. Human dignity would be the centerpiece of John Paul's writings and speeches, especially in his historic struggle with communism in Poland. In addition, he would become a nonviolent warrior for human rights around the globe.

A Larger Stage

Karol began to travel to the United States and Canada, Australia, New Zealand, the Philippines, and, of course, to Rome. By now he had become a favorite of Paul VI, and was asked to give the lenten retreat for the curia. Though the talks were heavy, the Vatican officials were impressed with Karol's holiness and breadth of knowledge.

Paul VI died in 1978 and John Paul I was elected. He died thirty-three days later. This year became known as the "year of the three popes." In the fall of that year a conclave was called once again and elected another pontiff.

A Polish Pope

Much to the world's surprise, a rather unknown young Polish cardinal was elected to the papacy, Karol Wojtyla. He took the name John Paul II and chose the motto *Totus tuus*, ("I am wholly yours"), indicating his life-long devotion to Mary, the mother of Jesus.

There was rejoicing in Poland when Wojtyla was elected to the papacy. Though the Poles regretted losing him as their cardinal, they knew that he would be a formidable force against the communist regime that held them captive. Of course, this was not good news for the Party officials. As one Italian paper noted, "The soviets would rather see [Aleksander] Solzhenitsyn made secretary-general of the UN, than a Pole become pope."[10]

John Paul early on made it clear to the communists in Poland and throughout the world that he would be a champion for human freedom. Josef Stalin had once sarcastically asked: "How many divisions has the pope?" Well, John Paul made it clear that he had no armored divisions, but that he had legions of people empowered with the Spirit of Jesus and that they would ultimately prevail over those who wanted to take away their freedom. In his inaugural sermon in 1978, he emboldened all those persecuted behind the Iron Curtain. He told them: "Be not afraid! Open the doors to Christ." He sent messages of hope to the churches in Czechoslovakia, the Ukraine, and Poland. In his meeting with the Soviet foreign minister, Andrei Gromyko, John Paul pointed out the there were obstacles to religious freedom in the U.S.S.R. It was clear that John Paul saw himself as "the Slav Pope," determined to free his people from communist rule.

In his first encyclical, The Redeemer of Man (March 1979), the new pope explained that Christ's redemption was linked to the dignity of the human person and that the church's mission was to defend this dignity. Humans are called to love, and freedom is necessary to express true love. Moreover, John Paul taught that true freedom is ordered to the truth and he insisted that religious freedom is the first of inalienable human rights. The church must have its freedom to carry out its mission of incarnating Jesus' love for all humanity.[11]

The Pope's First Pilgrimage to Poland
John Paul's return to his homeland was triumphant. Millions jubilantly heard his many addresses and attended his Masses. His message often

focused on human dignity that has been redeemed by Christ and how central that had been for Poland for a thousand years. His people had a right to that heritage. His prayer was that the Spirit would renew that face of his land, and everywhere his people chanted: "We want God!"

George Weigel, John Paul's biographer, noted that this visit made it clear: "Poland was not a communist country; Poland was a Catholic nation saddled with a communist state."[12] At the same time, he addressed the Czechs, Croatians, Slovenes, Bulgarians, and even Russians who had slipped into Poland for his visit, as well as others oppressed by the Soviets, that he would not forget them.[13] The pope was on a mission: to preach the message of human dignity, the value of the ethical over the technical, of the spiritual over the material from the Urals to the Atlantic.[14]

John Paul's visit gave his people a new sense of dignity and purpose. The people felt a new sense of courage: Strikes began to break out across Poland and unions were formed. The movement spread to the shipyards at Gdańsk, where a strike was led by Lech Walesa, and there were demands for a free trade union.

The Pope Supports Solidarity

John Paul sent a message of his support of the movement to a cautious hierarchy: "I pray that, once again, the Episcopate with the Primate at its head…may be able to aid the nation in its struggle for daily bread, social justice, and the safeguarding of its inviolable right to its own way of life and achievement."[15] The hierarchy had its marching orders and the workers had the support of their pope. The Solidarity movement had been born, was begrudgingly recognized by the communist regime, and a threatened Soviet invasion had been prevented.

The struggle was far from over and this became more apparent when the Soviets put Premier Wojciech Jaruzelski in to proclaim martial law and crush the unions. Solidarity leaders were beaten, and a national strike defied the regime. Once again the Soviets threatened invasion, but the pope's call for restraint and a series of compromises calmed the crisis. Clearly a peaceful counterrevolution was underway in Poland, inspired and supported by John Paul. At the same time, the communists were going to great lengths to crush the call to freedom. Solidarity had been suppressed, demonstrations forbidden, and Walesa had been imprisoned.

A Second Visit to Poland

In John Paul's second visit to Poland in 1983, he found his country more somber and discouraged. The crowds were smaller and a sense of cynicism was in the air. The pope offered a Mass in the cathedral where he compassionately reached out to his people knowing that their dignity had been trampled. The next morning he confronted Jaruzelski, who seemed to be intimidated, and urged him to recognize Solidarity and give Poland its independence. The regime was frightened into giving into labor demands and even agreed to allow the pope to meet with Walesa. The pope then held a Mass for three million people, pledging nonviolent resistance and his support for Solidarity. He continued this message of hope and encouragement throughout Poland, relentlessly calling for freedom and the recognition of human rights.

John Paul had once again enkindled hope in his people. Jaruzelski called for another meeting, but with the throngs cheering the pope outside, knew that he had lost the battle. The people believed in themselves and knew that it was only a matter of time before they would have their freedom.

Their pope and compatriot had told them: "Be not afraid!" In subsequent visits, he continued to give support to his beleaguered nation.

An Amazing Collapse

Poland struggled for freedom for several more years. In 1985 Mikhail Gorbachev took over the Soviet Union. He refused to send the army to intervene in the Soviet-bloc countries and one by one they chose freedom. Poland led the way with elections in 1989, Czechoslovakia in 1989, Eastern Germany and the amazing dismantling of the Berlin wall in 1989, and Hungary in 1990. By 1991, much to the whole world's amazement, the Soviet Union had come down like a house of cards. An arms race that bankrupted the U.S.S.R., the unrealized hopes for class equality, a corrupt economy, the violent suppression of human dignity and rights, and the deep human desire for freedom and religion had all contributed to what seemed like a sudden collapse of the Soviet Union. Of course, John Paul's untiring crusade for human rights and nonviolent resistance against tyranny had to be recognized as an important factor. As Gorbachev later acknowledged: "Everything that has happened in Eastern Europe in recent years would have been impossible without the efforts of the Pope."[16]

Peace and Justice in Other Areas
As the new millennium approached, nearly half of all Catholics would be Latin Americans, so John Paul had to be concerned about peace and justice in that area as well. Early in his papacy, he was concerned about the bishops of Latin America and their affiliation with liberation theology. At a meeting in Medellín, Colombia, in 1968, these bishops had abandoned the rich oligarchies and military regimes and taken the side of the poor, embracing liberation theology. When these bishops called another meeting in 1978 in Puebla, Mexico, to resolve the many thorny issues that had arisen over the last ten years, John Paul wanted to be there.

On the way, John Paul stopped at the Dominican Republic and spoke against the exploitation of the peasants, the corruption of the rich, and oppression of the poor. He made no effort to get involved in the very complicated political situation there. On the plane to Mexico, John Paul told reporters that liberation theology was not theology at all but a social program. He saw it as a front for communism.

The bishops arriving at Puebla were, for the most part, supporters of liberation theology and encouraged social activism. In El Salvador, Archbishop Oscar Romero had just excommunicated his president for the constant murder of priests and laypeople by the military. In Chile, the bishops struggled against the tyrant Augusto José Ramón Pinochet, who had killed thousands of political opponents. Priests, who were teaching that Jesus was a liberator and who were using the gospels in base communities to teach freedom, were being killed all over Central and South America.

From John Paul's point of view, liberation theology was Marxist, based on class struggle, and it encouraged the clergy to get involved in politics where they did not belong. He would simply not allow Jesus or his message to become politicized. For him, liberation had to come from conversion and an insistence on human dignity and human rights. There was never a place for violent revolution, which Paul VI had allowed in extreme cases.

John Paul spoke strongly against injustice and for liberation, but liberation from sin. This was his message as he continued to tour Mexico before adoring crowds, but at his meeting with the bishops he shocked them with his reading of their situation and the firmness of his position. Many wondered if the pontiff fully understood their situation. The Vatican remained hostile toward liberation theology, but eventually John Paul came to soften his views on some versions of this theology.[17] Though he had once opposed the positions of Archbishop Romero, John Paul later stopped at his tomb and paid homage.

In 1980 John Paul visited Brazil and supported the two Brazilian cardinals, Evaristo Arns and Alósio Lorscheider, who were struggling against a series of repressive military governments. When the pope addressed the crowds he criticized the government for its violence and abuse of rights. Speaking to young people, he encouraged them to transform the social structures that they found to be unjust and he told them that his own life in Poland had taught him that social justice could only be achieved when people recognized that humans are created in the image and likeness of God.[18] Everywhere he decried the subhuman conditions, the poverty and undernourishment, and as a gesture he took off his papal ring and donated it to the poor. He lectured his bishops to serve their people, but at the same time warned them to avoid ideology and involvement in political parties.

In 1983 John Paul came to Nicaragua, where the Sandinistas had overthrown an oppressive government, with the support of many clergy. The Reagan Administration in turn was funneling large sums of money to defeat the Sandinistas, believing them to be communists. It was a highly charged atmosphere when the pope landed in Managua on March 4. He rejected the greeting of a venerable monk-poet, Ernesto Cardenal, who was acting as the minister of culture, and scolded him publicly for his political involvement. At the Mass there was division between the official church and those who supported the Sandinistas. There was shouting and disruption during the Mass, as John Paul denounced the so-called "people's church" ideology and disobedience to the bishops. At one point the pope had to shout "Silence," and the whole liturgy ended on a sour note. John Paul said he had come to try to end the suffering of innocent people, end the conflict and hatred, and open the way to dialogue. Unfortunately, very little dialogue occurred on the visit.

In that same year John Paul visited Haiti, where dictator Jean-Claude (Baby Doc) Duvalier had been stripping his people of their money, starving them, forcing them to live in pitiful conditions, and terrorizing them with murderous voodoo witchdoctors. After a Mass with tens of thousands, John Paul denounced Duvalier to his face and rebuked him for how he had treated his people for twenty-five years. Three years later Duvalier was overthrown and exiled. Many think that John Paul's public denunciation played a key role in the corrupt dictator's demise.

In 1987 John Paul visited Chile and had another dictator in his sights, the infamous Augusto Pinochet. On the plane, John Paul bluntly told reporters that the regime was dictatorial and the church must work for the defense of human rights in Chile. Once in the country, the pope heard many stories of thousands tortured, killed, and disappeared. He endorsed the work of the bishops and priests for justice. At the main event Mass, the pope brought forth many witnesses to the atrocities. The government reacted with tear gas, water cannons, and buckshot. The pope remained calm, finished the service and was led off coughing from tear gas. The people and the clergy now felt emboldened by the support of John Paul. Eighteen months later Pinochet offered a plebiscite and his rule was rejected by the people. John Paul then proceeded in his fearless defense of human dignity and rights in the Philippines and Argentina and indeed in every corner of the world.

Key Writings on Justice
John Paul's first encyclical, The Redeemer of Man (1979), was concerned with human dignity, human rights, and religious freedom. He ex-pounded on his perennial theme, that every person is a living image of God and shares in Jesus' mission of love. This calls Christians to sacrifice, even lay down their lives for one another. The church stands in the world as a sacramental sign of this love and sacrifice. Social action is indeed part of God's plan![19] For him, "development" must go beyond materialism and extend to the social, cultural, and spiritual dimensions of people. He urges that the wealth of the Northern Hemisphere be shared with the South.[20] It was the Pontiff's conviction that the poverty of the developing world was a result of the struggle between liberal capitalism and communism, and he was critical of both systems and thought both extremes drifted toward imperialism.

In his encyclical The Hundredth Year, John Paul reiterated his signature Christian notion of the human person, as revealed in God's creation, the incarnation, and redemption of Jesus Christ. The vision of the human person in Christ is one of goodness, truth, love, and sacrifice. Herein lies the basis for the church's mission for social justice, a mission that is derived from the gospels themselves. He maintained that atheistic communism and capitalistic consumerism deny this anthropology: The first denies the spiritual dimension of the human; the second leads to a destructive selfishness. John Paul here tempered his earlier comments of capitalism and placed his hope in democracies with fair free market economies.[21]

Conclusions

Karol Wojtyla, John Paul II, leaves behind an enormous personal and ecclesial legacy. In his early struggles with the Nazis and then the communists, he found his own humanity and that of others as imaged in God, shaped by Jesus, and saved in crucifixion and resurrection.

Called to the priesthood, the episcopacy, and then to the papacy, he shared his vision of the human person with the people of his country and indeed with the world in tireless efforts to defend human dignity and the nonviolent struggle for peace and justice. Even in his final years, crippled and in poor health, he strongly opposed America's invasion of Iraq. To the very end he was a witness to gospel love, justice, and nonviolence.

notes

Chapter One: Jean Donovan

1. Joanne Turpin, *Women in Church History: 21 Stories for 21 Centuries* (Cincinnati: St. Anthony Messenger Press, 2007), p. 202.
2. Ana Carrigan, *Salvador Witness: The Life and Calling of Jean Donovan* (New York: Simon and Schuster, 1984), p. 67.
3. Turpin, p. 192.
4. Carrigan, p. 99.
5. Robert Royal, *The Catholic Martyrs of the Twentieth Century: A Comprehensive World History* (New York: Crossroad, 2000), p. 298.
6. Carrigan, p. 107.
7. Carrigan, p. 115.
8. Carrigan, p. 159.
9. Carrigan, p. 162.
10. For more on Sister Carla, see Judith M. Noone, M.M., *The Same Fate as the Poor* (Maryknoll, N.Y.: Maryknoll Sisters Publication, 1984), pp. 9–18.
11. Carrigan, pp. 190, 193.
12. For an account of the accident, see Jeanne Evans, ed. *"Here I Am Lord": The Letters and Writings of Ita Ford* (Maryknoll, N.Y.: Orbis, 2005), pp. 202–217.
13. Royal, p. 299.
14. Carrigan, p. 218.
15. Carrigan, p. 218.
16. Raymond Bonner, *Weakness and Deceit: U.S. Policy and El Salvador* (New York: Times, 1984), p. 137.
17. Carrigan, p. 231.
18. Carrigan, p. 243.
19. Robert Armstrong and Janet Shenk, *El Salvador: The Face of Revolution* (Boston: South End, 1982), p. 175.
20. Jon Sobrino, *Witnesses to the Kingdom* (Maryknoll, N.Y.: Orbis, 2003), p. 54.
21. For more details, see Phyllis Zagano, *Ita Ford: Missionary Martyr* (New York: Paulist, 1996), pp. 39–44.
22. Enrique Baloyra, *El Salvador in Transition* (Chapel Hill, N.C.: University of North Carolina Press, 1982), p. 115.
23. Carrigan, p. 261.
24. Bonner, p. 79.
25. Sobrino, p. 55.

26. Carrigan, p. 279.
27. Bonner, p. 76.
28. *The New York Times*, Nov. 4, 2002.
29. Carrigan, p. 30.

Chapter Two: Sister Helen Prejean, C.S.J.
1. Helen Prejean, C.S.J., *Dead Man Walking: An Eyewitness Account of the Death Penalty in the United States* (New York: Vintage, 1993), p. 95.
2. Carol Lee Flinders, *Enduring Lives: Portraits of Women and Faith in Action* (New York: Penguin, 2006), p. 268.
3. Flinders, p. 270.
4. Flinders, p. 270.
5. Flinders, p. 277. See Helen Prejean, *The Death of Innocents: An Eyewitness Account of Wrongful Executions* (New York: Vintage, 2005), p. 179.
6. Prejean, *Dead Man Walking*, p. 11.
7. Prejean, *Dead Man Walking*, p. 22.
8. Prejean, *Dead Man Walking*, p. 47.
9. Flinders, p. 292.
10. Prejean, *Dead Man Walking*, pp. 88–89.
11. Prejean, *Dead Man Walking*, p. 99.
12. Prejean, *Dead Man Walking*, p. 149.
13. Prejean, *Dead Man Walking*, p. 179.
14. Helen Prejean, "The Upward Mobility of the Gospel," *Voices of the Religious Left,* Rebecca T. Alpert, ed. (Philadelphia: Temple University Press, 2000), p. 179.
15. Prejean, *Dead Man Walking*, p. 117.
16. Prejean, *The Death of Innocents,* p. 217.
17. Prejean, *Dead Man Walking*, pp. 43–46.
18. Prejean, *Dead Man Walking*, p. 233.
19. Prejean, *Dead Man Walking*, pp. 114–15.
20. Prejean, *The Death of Innocents*, p. 184.
21. Prejean, *The Death of Innocents*, p. 188.
22. Prejean, *The Death of Innocents*, p. 262.
23. Prejean, *The Death of Innocents*, p, 184.
24. Prejean, *The Death of Innocents*, p. 118.
25. Prejean, *The Death of Innocents*, pp. 132–133.
26. Prejean, *The Death of Innocents*, p. 170.
27. Prejean, *The Death of Innocents*, pp. 270–71.

Chapter Three: Sister Dorothy Stang, S.N.D. DE N
1. See the DVD documentary *The Student, the Nun and the Amazon* (2005)

by James Newton and Sam Clements, available at www.studentnun amazon.com.

2. Binka Le Breton, *The Greatest Gift: The Courageous Life and Martyrdom of Sister Dorothy Stang* (New York: Doubleday, 2007), p. 20.
3. Breton, p. 32.
4. Roseanne Murphy, *Martyr of the Amazon: The Life of Sister Dorothy Stang* (Maryknoll, N.Y.: Orbis, 2007), p. 5.
5. Breton, pp. 42–43.
6. Murphy, p. 16.
7. Murphy, p. 23.
8. Breton, p. 59.
9. Breton, pp. 66–67.
10. Breton, p. 76.
11. Breton, pp. 121–22.
12. Murphy, p. 103.
13. Breton, p. 126.
14. Murphy, pp. 96–97.
15. Murphy, p. 95.
16. Murphy, p. 106.
17. Murphy, p. 116.
18. Murphy, p. 113.
19. Murphy, p. 122.
20. Murphy, p. 131.
21. Murphy, p. 139.
22. Murphy, p. 142.
23. Murphy, p. 151.
24. Murphy, p. 155.
25. Murphy, pp. 158 ff.
26. Dan Shapley, "Injustice in the Amazon: The Once-Convicted Mastermind of American Nun's Murder is Acquitted," *The Daily Green*, May 8, 2008, p. 1.
27. Rich Heffern. "Suspected 'Mastermind' of Sr. Dorothy Stang's Murder Charged," *National Catholic Reporter*, January 9, 2009, p. 5.
28. Breton, p. xv.

Chapter Four: Father Pedro Arrupe, S.J.

1. George Bishop, *Pedro Arrupe, S.J.* (Anand, India: Gujarat Sahitya Prakash, 2000), p. 39.
2. Jerome Aixala, S.J., ed., *Pedro Arrupe, S.J.: Other Apostolates Today: Selected Letters and Addresses* (St. Louis: The Institute of Jesuit Resources, 1981), volume III, p. xiv.

3. Bishop, p. 46.
4. Aixala, III, p. xiv.
5. Bishop, p. 113 ff.
6. Bishop, pp. 10–56.
7. Pedro Arrupe, *A Planet to Heal: Reflections and Forecasts* (Rome: International Center for Jesuit Education, 1977), p. 25.
8. Bishop, p. 223.
9. Yolanda T. De Mola, trans., *Recollections and Reflections of Pedro Arrupe, S.J.* (Wilmington, Del.: Michael Glazier, 1986), p. 162.
10. De Mola, pp. 164–165.
11. Bishop, p. 247.
12. See complete commentary on the 1971 Synod of Bishops in *Modern Catholic Social Teaching: Commentaries and Interpretations,* eds. Kenneth Himes, O.F.M., et al. (Washington, D.C.: Georgetown University Press, 2005), p. 342.
13. Aixala, volume II, p. 95.
14. Aixala, volume II, p. 134.
15. Aixala, volume II, pp. 166–167.

Chapter Five: Thomas Merton
1. Michael Mott, *The Seven Mountains of Thomas Merton* (Boston: Houghton Mifflin, 1984), p. 65.
2. Mott, p. 100.
3. Mott, p. 139.
4. Mott, p. 169.
5. Mott, p. 172.
6. William H. Shannon, ed., *The Hidden Ground of Love: The Letters of Thomas Merton on Religious Experience and Social Concerns* (New York: Farrar, Straus and Giroux, 1985), p. 11.
7. Shannon, p. 12.
8. Mott, p. 304.
9. Mott, p. 315.
10. Mott, p. 311.
11. Thomas Merton, *Passion for Peace: Reflections on War and Nonviolence* (New York: Crossroad, 1950), p. 148.
12. Merton, *Passion for Peace,* pp. 276–86.
13. Thomas Merton, *Conjectures of a Guilty Bystander* (Garden City, N.Y.: Doubleday, 1966), pp. 219–220.
14. Merton, *Passion for Peace,* p. 11.
15. Merton, *Passion for Peace,* p. 13.

16. Merton, *Passion for Peace*, p. 19.
17. Anthony T. Padovano, *The Human Journey: Thomas Merton: Symbol of a Century* (Garden City, N.Y.: Doubleday, 1982), p. 68.
18. Merton, *Passion for Peace*, pp. 211–227.
19. Merton, *Passion for Peace*, pp. 263–269.
20. Thomas P. McDonnell, *A Thomas Merton Reader* (Garden City, N.Y.: Doubleday, 1974), p. 281.
21. Ronald G. Musto, *The Catholic Peace Tradition* (Maryknoll, N.Y.: Orbis, 1986), p. 250.
22. Musto, p. 251.
23. Merton, *Passion for Peace*, p. 36.
24. Merton, *Passion for Peace*, p. 47.
25. Merton, *Passion for Peace,* p. 63.
26. Merton, *Passion for Peace*, p. 65.
27. Jim Wallis and Joyce Hollyday, *Cloud of Witnesses* (Maryknoll, N.Y.: Orbis, 2005), p. 251.
28. Merton, *Passion for Peace*, p. 24.
29. Merton, *The Hidden Ground of Love*, p. 145.
30. Merton, *Conjectures of a Guilty Bystander*, p. 71.
31. Merton, *Conjectures of a Guilty Bystander*, p. 72.
32. Merton, *Conjectures of a Guilty Bystander*, p. 88.
33. Thomas Merton, "Blessed are the Meek: The Roots of Christian Nonviolence," *Peace is the Way: Writings on Nonviolence from the Fellowship of Reconciliation,* Walter Wink, ed. (Maryknoll, N.Y.: Orbis, 2000), p. 41.
34. Padovano, *The Human Journey*, p. 7.
35. Wallis and Hollyday, *Cloud of Witnesses*, p. 7.
36. Wink, *Peace is the Way*, pp. 43–45.
37. Thomas Merton*, Peace in the Post-Christian Era* (Maryknoll, N.Y.: Orbis, 2004), p. 29.
38. Musto, p. 251.
39. Gordon Zahn, "The Challenge of Conscience," *Peacemaking*, Gerard F. Powers, et al., eds. (Washington, D.C.: USCCB, 1994), p. 201.
40. Shannon, *The Hidden Ground of Love*, pp. 86, 281.
41. Shannon, *The Hidden Ground of Love*, p. 439.
42. Merton, *Passion for Peace*, pp. 315–321.

Chapter Six: Father Maximilian Kolbe, O.F.M
1. Desmond Forristal, *Kolbe: A Saint in Auschwitz* (New Rochelle, N.Y.: Don Bosco, 1982), p. 174.
2. Forristal, pp. 52–53.

3. Forristal, pp. 53–54.
4. Forristal, p. 59.
5. Forristal, p. 61.
6. Patricia Treece, *A Man for Others: Maximilian Kolbe, Saint of Auschwitz* (Huntington, Ind: Our Sunday Visitor, 1982), p. 59. See also Francis Kavelage, ed., *Kolbe: Saint of Immaculata* (New Bedford, Mass.: Franciscans of the Immaculate, 2001), p. 203 ff.
7. Treece, p. 66.
8. Elaine Murray Stone, *Maximilian Kolbe: Saint of Auschwitz* (New York: Paulist, 1997), pp. 58–59.
9. Andre Frossard, *"Forget Not Love: The Passion of Maximilian Kolbe* (San Francisco: Ignatius, 1987), p. 9.
10. Frossard, p. 165.
11. Frossard, p. 166.
12. Boniface Hanley, O.F.M., *Maximilian Kolbe: No Greater Love* (Notre Dame, Ind.: Ave Maria, 1982), p. 62.
13. Frossard, pp. 76–77.
14. Frossard, p. 180.
15. Hanley, pp. 62–63.
16. Hanley, p. 65.
17. Hanley, p. 63.
18. Hanley, p. 66.
19. Forristal, p.160.
20. Forristal, p. 180. See Paul Mariani, "Maxilimilian Kolbe," *Martyrs,* Susan Bergman, ed. (Maryknoll, N.Y.: Orbis 1996), p. 229.
21. Forristal, p. 181.

Chapter Seven: Cardinal Joseph Bernardin
1. Eugene Kennedy, *Bernardin: Life to the Full* (Chicago: Bonus, 1997) p. 345.
2. Tim Unsworth, *I Am Your Brother Joseph* (New York: Crossroad, 1997), p. 94.
3. Kennedy, p. 27.
4. Unsworth, p. 56.
5. Kennedy, p. 28.
6. Unsworth, p. 13.
7. Kennedy, pp. 111–112.
8. Unsworth, p. 59.
9. Cardinal Joseph Bernardin, *The Gift of Peace: Personal Reflections* (Chicago: Loyola, 1997), p. 6.
10. See Genesis 45:4.

11. Alphonse P. Spilly, C.PP.S., ed., *Selected Works of Joseph Cardinal Bernardin: Volume 2, Church and Society* (Collegeville, Minn.: Liturgical, 2000), p. 45.
12. Spilly, p. 44.
13. Spilly, p. 49.
14. Maximilian Heim, *Joseph Ratzinger: Life in the Church and Living Theology* (Fort Collins, Colo.: Ignatius, 2007), p. 495.
15. Gerald Powers, et al., eds., *Peacemaking: Moral and Policy Challenges for a New World* (Washington, D.C.: USCCB, 1994), p. 19
16. Powers, p. 25.
17. Spilly, p. 23.
18. Spilly, p. 25.
19. Spilly, p. 88.
20. Spilly, p. 88.
21. Spilly, p. 88.
22. Joseph Cardinal Bernardin, "A Consistent Ethic of Life and the Death Penalty in Our Time," *Capital Punishment,* Glen H. Stassen, ed. (Cleveland: Pilgrim, 1997), p. 154.
23. Spilly, p. 260.
24. *A Blessing to Each Other: Cardinal Joseph Bernardin and Jewish-Catholic Dialogue* (Chicago: Liturgical Training Publications, 1996), pp. 47, 51.
25. *A Blessing to Each Other*, p. 133.
26. Bernardin, *The Gift of Peace*, p. 23.
27. Bernardin, *The Gift of Peace*, p. 23.
28. Bernardin, *The Gift of Peace*, p. 93.
29. For further information on this initiative see *Catholic Common Ground Initiative: Foundational Documents* by Joseph Bernardin and Oscar Lipscomb (Eugene, Ore: Wipf & Stock, 2002).
30. Peter Steinfels, "Cardinal Bernardin Says He Has Inoperable Cancer," *The New York Times,* August 31, 1996.
31. Richard McBrien, "Obama's singling out Bernardin, Hesburgh is message for us," *National Catholic Reporter*, May 19, 2009.

Chapter Eight: Pope John Paul II
1. Garry O'Connor, *Universal Father: A Life of Pope John Paul II* (New York: Bloomsbury, 2005), p. 6.
2. George Weigel, *Witness to Hope: The Biography of Pope John Paul II* (New York: Cliff Street, 1999), p. 65.
3. John Cornwell, *The Pontiff in Winter: Triumph and Conflict in the Reign of John Paul II* (New York: Random House, 2004), p. 33.
4. Cornwell, p. 34.
5. Weigel, p. 77.

6. Catherine Pepinster, ed., *John Paul II* (London: Barnes and Oates, 2005), p. 26.
7. O'Connor, p. 166.
8. Weigel, p. 192.
9. Weigel, p. 233.
10. O'Connor, p. 198.
11. Weigel, pp. 289–290.
12. Weigel, p. 295.
13. Jonathan Kwitny, *Man of the Century: The Life and Times of Pope John Paul II* (New York: Henry Holt, 1997), p. 326.
14. Kwitny, p. 361.
15. Weigel, p. 401.
16. Pepinster, p. 44.
17. Kwitny, pp. 518–519.
18. Kwitny, p. 366.
19. Gerard Beigel, *Faith and Social Justice in the Teaching of Pope John Paul II* (New York: Peter Lang, 1997), pp. 94, 97.
20. Avery Dulles, *The Splendor of Faith: The Theological Vision of Pope John Paul II* (New York: Herder and Herder, 1999), p. 138. See also Samuel Gregg, *Challenging the Modern World: Karol Wojtyla/John Paul II and the Development of Catholic Social Teaching* (New York: Lexington, 1999), pp. 203 ff.
21. Tim Perry, ed., *The Legacy of John Paul II* (Downers Grove, Ill.: Intervarsity, 2007), p. 242 ff. See also Carl Bernstein and Marco Politi, *His Holiness* (New York: Doubleday, 1996), p. 534 ff.

bibliography

Aixala, Jerome, s.j., ed. *Pedro Arrupe, s.j.: Other Apostolates Today: Selected Letters and Addresses.* St. Louis: The Institute of Jesuit Resources, 1981.

Armstrong, Robert, and Janet Shenk. *El Salvador: The Face of Revolution.* Boston: South End, 1982.

Arrupe, Pedro. *A Planet to Heal: Reflections and Forecasts.* Rome: International Center for Jesuit Education, 1977.

————. *Recollections and Reflections of Pedro Arrupe, s.j.* Translated by Yolanda T. De Mola. Wilmington. Del: Michael Glazier, 1986.

Baloyra, Enrique. *El Salvador in Transition.* Chapel Hill, N.C.: The University of North Carolina Press, 1982.

Beigel, Gerard. *Faith and Social Justice in the Teaching of Pope John Paul II.* New York: Peter Lang, 1997.

Bernardin, Cardinal Joseph. "A Consistent Ethic of Life and the Death Penalty in Our Time," *Capital Punishment.* Edited by Glen H. Stassen. Cleveland: Pilgrim, 1997.

————. *The Gift of Peace: Personal Reflections.* Chicago: Loyola, 1997.

Bernstein, Carl and Marco Politi. *His Holiness.* New York: Doubleday, 1996.

Bishop, George. *Pedro Arrupe, s.j.* Anand, India: Gujarat Sahitya Prakash, 2000.

Bonner, Raymond. *Weakness and Deceit: U.S. Policy and El Salvador.* New York: Times, 1984.

Carrigan, Ana. *Salvador Witness.* New York: Simon and Schuster, 1984.

Cornwell, John. *The Pontiff in Winter: Triumph and Conflict in the Reign of John Paul II.* New York: Random House, 2004.

Dulles, Avery. *The Splendor of Faith: The Theological Vision of Pope John Paul II.* New York: Herder and Herder, 1999.

Evans, Jeanne. *"Here I Am Lord": The Letters and Writings of Ita Ford.* Maryknoll, N.Y.: Orbis, 2005.

Flinders, Carol Lee. *Enduring Lives: Portraits of Women and Faith in Action.* New York: Penguin, 2006.

Forristal, Desmond. *Kolbe: A Saint in Auschwitz.* New Rochelle, N.Y.: Don Bosco, 1982.

Frossard, Andre. *"Forget Not Love": The Passion of Maximilian Kolbe.* San Francisco: Ignatius, 1987.

Gregg, Samuel. *Challenging the Modern World: Karol Wojtyla/John Paul II and the Development of Catholic Social Teaching.* New York: Lexington, 1999.

Hanley, Boniface. O.F.M. *Maximilian Kolbe: No Greater Love.* Notre Dame, Ind.: Ave Maria, 1982.

Heim, Maximilian. *Joseph Ratzinger: Life in the Church and Living Theology.* Fort Collins, Colo.: Ignatius, 2007.

Himes, Kenneth, O.F.M., et al., eds. *Modern Catholic Social Teaching: Commentaries and Interpretations.* Washington, D.C.: Georgetown University Press, 2005.

Hollyday, Joyce and Jim Wallis. *Cloud of Witnesses.* Maryknoll, N.Y.: Orbis, 2005.

Kennedy, Eugene. *Bernardin: Life to the Full.* Chicago: Bonus, 1997.

Kwitny, Jonathan. *Man of the Century: The Life and Times of Pope John Paul II.* New York: Henry Holt, 1997.

Le Breton, Binka. *The Greatest Gift: The Courageous Life and Martyrdom of Sister Dorothy Stang.* New York: Doubleday, 2007.

McDonnell, Thomas. *A Thomas Merton Reader.* Garden City, N.Y.: Doubleday, 1974.

Merton, Thomas. "Blessed are the Meek: The Roots of Christian Nonviolence," *Peace Is the Way.* Edited by Walter Wink. Maryknoll, N.Y.: Orbis, 2000.

———. *Conjectures of a Guilty Bystander.* Garden City, N.Y.: Doubleday, 1966.

———. *Passion for Peace: Reflections on War and Nonviolence.* New York: Crossroad, 1950.

———. *Peace in the Post-Christian Era.* Maryknoll, N.Y.: Orbis Books, 2004.

Mott, Michael. *The Seven Mountains of Thomas Merton.* Boston: Houghton Mifflin, 1984.

Murphy, Roseanne. *Martyr of the Amazon: The Life of Sister Dorothy Stang* Maryknoll, N.Y.: Orbis, 2007.

Musto, Ronald, G. *The Catholic Peace Tradition.* Maryknoll, N.Y.; Orbis Books, 1986.

Noone, Judith M., M.M. *The Same Fate as the Poor.* Maryknoll, N.Y.: Maryknoll, 1984.

O'Connor, Garry. *Universal Father: A Life of Pope John Paul II.* New York: Bloomsbury, 2005.

Padovano, Anthony. T. *The Human Journey: Thomas Merton: Symbol of a Century.* Garden City, N.Y.: Doubleday, 1982.

Pepinster, Catherine, ed. *John Paul II.* London: Burns and Oates, 2005.

Perry, Tim, ed. *The Legacy of John Paul II.* Downers Grove, Ill.: Intervarsity, 2007.

Powers, Gerald, et al., eds. *Peacemaking: Moral and Policy Challenges for a New World.* Washington, D.C.: USCCB, 1994.

Prejean, Helen. *Dead Man Walking: An Eyewitness Account of the Death Penalty in the United States.* New York: Vintage, 1993.

————. *The Death of Innocents: An Eyewitness Account of Wrongful Executions.* New York: Vintage, 2005.

————. "The Upward Mobility of the Gospel," *Voices of the Religious Left.* Edited by Rebecca T. Alpert. Philadelphia: Temple University Press, 2000.

Royal, Robert. *The Catholic Martyrs of the Twentieth Century: A Comprehensive World History.* New York: Crossroad, 2000.

Shannon, William H., ed. *The Hidden Ground of Love: The Letters of Thomas Merton on Religious Experience and Social Concerns.* New York: Farrar, Straus and Giroux, 1985.

Sobrino, Jon. *Witnesses to the Kingdom.* Maryknoll, N.Y.: Orbis, 2003.

Spilly, Alphonse P., ed. *Selected Works of Joseph Cardinal Bernardin: Volume 2, Church and Society.* Collegeville, Minn.: Liturgical, 2000.

Stone, Elaine Murray. *Maximilian Kolbe: Saint of Auschwitz.* New York: Paulist, 1997.

Treece, Patricia. *A Man for Others: Maximilian Kolbe, Saint of Auschwitz.* Huntington, Ind.: Our Sunday Visitor, 1982.

Turpin, Joanne. *Women in Church History: 21 Stories for 21 Centuries.* Cincinnati: St. Anthony Messenger Press, 2007.

Unsworth, Tim. *I Am Your Brother Joseph.* New York: Crossroad, 1997.

Weigel, George. *Witness to Hope: The Biography of Pope John Paul II.* New York: Cliff Street, 1999.

Zagano, Phyllis. *Ita Ford: Missionary Martyr.* New York: Paulist, 1996.

Zahn, Gordan. "The Challenge of Conscience," *Peacemaking.* Edited by Gerard F. Powers, et al. Washington, D.C.: USCCB, 1994.

index

About the Author

BRENNAN R. HILL, PH.D., is professor emeritus in the theology department at Xavier University in Cincinnati. His most recent books are *8 Freedom Heroes: Changing the World with Faith; 8 Spiritual Heroes: Their Search for God; Jesus the Christ: Contemporary Perspectives* (New Edition) and *The On-Going Renewal of Catholicism.*